When Baseball was King
The New York Yankees were King of Baseball

When Baseball was King
The New York Yankees were King of Baseball

Dr. Len Bergantino, Ed.D., Ph.D.

InfusedMedia Co. LLC
www.infusedmedia.co
1-888-251-6088

DEDICATION

This book is dedicated to "Mike Smith" who insisted I write about baseball!

Books that are either published or will be published authored by The Reverend Dr. Len Bergantino as these books were written as the thing-in itself and were divinely inspired by the Holy Spirit to at the very least give men and women an opportunity to be more fully themselves and more in touch with their own nature. It is strongly recommended that the readers develop their level of attention to read all four books and permit them to become part parcel of how each individual answers the question "TO BE OR NOT TO BE". As The Reverend Dr. Len Bergantino is seventy five years old, he will not be around personally to do psychoanalysis or psychotherapy with you, therefore these books were written on the basis of them being around for at least TWO HUNDRED YEARS!!!

1. I AM FREUD! PSYCHOANALYSIS IS THE ONLY METHOD OF CURE: IT'S TOO BAD NO ONE KNOWS HOW TO DO ONE, XLIBRIS PUB. CO., 2019. 502 PP.
2. REVERSE ANALYSIS, THE EXISTENTIAL SHIFT, GESTALT FAMILY THERAPY AND THE PREVENTION OF THE HOLOCAUST, XLIBRIS PUB. CO,
3. THE ART OF PSYCHOTHERAPY AND THE LIBERATION OF THE THERAPIST XLIBRIS PUBLISHING COMPANY.
4. THE ESSENCE OF MUSIC, XLIBRIS PUBLISHING COMPANY.

This is a book for all time. As I had extrasensory perception to help me find out things on a primitive level and depth with an ability to pick up split-off, severe pathological projective identifications moment to moment in an era when psychologists were only permitted to be research psychoanalysts by the American Psychoanalytic Association (but rightly controlled where that research was going that in many ways nullified it as true psychoanalytic research). I present to you a book that might at that time have been considered wild psychoanalysis. And I will show you how extrasensory perception can be developed and utilized by the therapeutic use of self within the psychoanalytic frame in ways that can enhance the treatment of borderline, narcissistic, obsessive-compulsive, and schizophrenic disorders and other diagnoses, as well as help pinpoint psychophysiological awareness, which through the repetition-compulsion, can prevent disease and will circumvent disease in later life. This kind of psychoanalysis will go a long way in preventing the next holocaust!

Dr. Bergantino and his two children were sent back on a karmic mission to complete the work. Dr. Bergantino is the reincarnated soul of Sigmund Freud and Julius Caesar. Those skill sets were required to complete this project. His children are Wilfred Bion and Milton Erickson. They taught Dr. Bergantino how to use paranormal abilities. We are all off the karmic wheel and WE WILL NOT BE BACK!!! GOODBYE!!

Xlibris

TO PURCHASE THIS 502 pp. BOOK GO TO
www. Xlibris . com and type in either the
title of the book or. Dr. Len Bergantino,
or contact barnes and noble.com
or amazon.com

Xlibris

I DARED TO DISTURB THE UNIVERSE!!!

Dr. Len Bergantino Ed. D., Ph.D., releases 'I AM Freud! Psychoanalysis Is the Only Method of Cure: It's Too Bad No One Knows How to Do One!!!'

BEVERLY HILLS, Calif. – Dr. Len Bergantino, Ed.D., Ph.D., is the reincarnated soul of Sigmund Freud and Julius Caesar and his children Lisa Francesca is the reincarnated soul of the great British psychoanalyst Wilfred R. Bion and Cleopatra while his developmentally delayed son Alexander Leonardo is the reincarnated soul of Milton H. Erickson, M.D. (known as the father of Modern Medical Hypnosis and for Uncommon Therapy) and Decimus Brutus. All of those skill sets were necessary in the writing of "I Am Freud! Psychoanalysis Is the Only Method of Cure: It's Too Bad No One Knows How to Do One!!!" (published by Xlibris) and the issues it is meant to deal with at both conscious and unconscious levels.

Further, Bergantino in 1980, made a direct contact with God to have Bion and Erickson sent back as the reincarnated souls of his children to teach him what to do with the paranormal gifts that were given to him and unleashed by Erickson. Through this development, he, with God's tutelage became the best psychoanalyst that ever lived and began to implement Freud's plan that both psychoanalysis and subsequently developed psychotherapies would create the kind of patients who would and could then go out and create an upward spiraling society.

Wilhelm Reich, M.D. – Freud's most gifted training analyst said "If you can't do politics, you can't do analysis!" The book shows how to develop extrasensory perception so that analysts and therapists have an opportunity to develop the tools necessary to do the jobs at hand if they are so inclined. In this way, people will not pay for a five day a week, seven year analysis and come out as crazy as the day they began with few if any tools to carry on the work. "When I did an analysis with the crème de la crème of society, they customarily tripled their income and the quality of their life! (Don't waste $50,000 per year or $350,000 per analysis)."

The book is not based on anything Bergantino may or may not believe. It is based on his attaining a level of "pure being" that Jean Paul Sartre wrote about as the thing-in-itself. And it is at that level that this book was written as the thing-in-itself to effect change in the reader.

"I Am Freud! Psychoanalysis Is the Only Method of Cure: It's Too Bad No One Knows How to Do One!!!"
By Dr. Len Bergantino, Ed.D., Ph.D.
Hardcover | 6 x 9in | 504 pages | ISBN 9781984557308
Softcover | 6 x 9in | 504 pages | ISBN 9781984557292
E-Book | 504 pages | ISBN 9781984557285
Available at www.amazon.com and www.barnesandnoble.com

About the Author

Dr. Len Bergantino, Ed.D., Ph.D. practiced psychoanalysis in Beverly Hills, California from 1979-1991. He saw seven patients five days a week for between five and seven years totalling 49 hours a week and saw an occasional family therapy or clinical hypnosis case totaling 52 hours a week at $125 per hour; $625 per week; $240,000 per year. In addition, he trained psychiatrists and clinical psychologists at the international level delivering on his workshop promise "The Therapeutic Wizardry of Dr. Len Bergantino" at Wentworth Castle in Sheffield, England and training the British at the Royal College of Medicine in London in "Developing the Use of Extrasensory Perception in the Practice of Psychoanalysis, Psychotherapy and Clinical Hypnosis." In Brisbane, Australia, his work was described as "a kind of mental precision" that electrified the Australian Therapeutic Community and had lasting therapeutic impact. Furthermore, he was an affiliate of the Italian American Lawyers Association for seven years. He became an expert witness in both severe parental Alienation Syndrome in criminal cases. He was the only clinician to plea bargain a man for release who was on death row. He was President of the Southern California Society of Clinical Hypnosis when they were composed of exclusively MD's, PHD's and DDS'. The year he was president he turned it into a psychoanalytic institute.

###

About the Author

Dr. Len Bergantino, Ed.D., Ph.D.

The Reverend Dr. Len Bergantino was trained in psychoanalysis including the personnial and ordinary methods of training by Dr. Wilfred R. Bion MCRS (Medical Royal College of Surgeons). Many of Bion's M.D. Analysands in Beverly Hills, CA, Dr. Martin Grotjahn, M.D. and Dr. Bruno Bettelheim, Ph.D. who was in Freud's original training group. These were all Training Analysts. Dr. Michael Paul M.D. is one of the last best of Bion's Training Analysands.

x

REVERSE ANALYSIS, THE EXISTENTIAL SHIFT, GESTALT FAMILY THERAPY AND THE PREVENTION OF THE NEXT HOLOCAUST

Dr. Leo Berjantino, E.D., Ph.D.

Xlibris

ISBN 978-1-7960-4517-3

6.00 x 9.00
(229 mm x 152 mm)

Content Type: Black & White
Paper Type: Creme
Page Count: 264
File Type: InDesign
Request ID: CSS0000000

"FOR IMMEDIATE RELEASE"

EDITORS: For review copies or interview requests, contact:
Marketing Services
Tel: 888-795-4274
Fax: 812-355-4079
Email: MarketingServices@xlibrisdesi.com
(When requesting a review copy, please provide a street address.)

Dr. Len Bergantino, Ed.D., Ph.D., addresses societal issues in new book

'Reverse Analysis, the Existential Shift, Gestalt Family Therapy and the Prevention of the Next Holocaust' released

LOS ANGELES – Through the Holy Spirit, his direct contact with God and his karmic mission, Dr. Len Bergantino, Ed.D., Ph.D., addresses the problem of the today's downward spiraling society in his latest book "Reverse Analysis, the Existential Shift, Gestalt Family Therapy and the Prevention of the Next Holocaust" (published by Xlibris).

This book creates a subliminal methodology that will help to prevent the next holocaust and perhaps deter the apocalypse and the end of days. As such, the book expands and enriches the community standards of practice of Psychoanalysis, psychiatry, clinical psychology, politics, political intervention and a realliance of religion with the state, as opposed to a separation of church and state that has left its people a soulless and emotionally bankrupt nation with a downward spiraling society. This book throws the United States government and its citizens into an international pot of family therapy as evoked at the unconscious and primitive levels required to effect and affect societal change, to evolve a redirection to an upward spiraling society providing the kind of leadership for Americans to create well-being and prosperity for all.

"[The book] is the common man's best shot to turn the tragic corner in his or her life: make dysfunctional families functional; save one's soul; become thoughtful members of society who do the right thing more often than not," Bergantino says. "This book also trains therapists how to do one session existential shifts thereby creating therapies for the common man that are more affordable than a seven year psychoanalysis where the patient is seen five days a week. In other words, it makes the currently impossible possible!"

At its core, the book aims to remind readers to "Open up the space and keep it open so Man will not destroy himself via the illusion of safety and will learn to experientially tolerate the anxiety and chaos of not knowing."

"Reverse Analysis, the Existential Shift, Gestalt Family Therapy and the Prevention of the Next Holocaust"
By Dr. Len Bergantino, Ed.D., Ph.D.
Hardcover | 6 x 9in | 244 pages | ISBN 9781796021189
Softcover | 6 x 9in | 244 pages | ISBN 9781796021172
E-Book | 244 pages | ISBN 9781796021165
Available at Amazon and Barnes & Noble

About the Author

Dr. Len Bergantino, Ed.D., Ph.D., has written THE HOLY BIBLE OF Psychoanalysis, psychotherapy, political psychology and music-books, I-IV!!! The books are the thing-in-itself and all four books must be read to make the necessary personal and societal impact!!! He was trained by Milton Erickson, M.D., Carl Whitaker, M.D., Wilfred Bion, M.R.C.S., Walter Kempler, M.D., George Bach, Ph.D., Bruno Bettelheim, Ph.D., Jim Simkin, Ph.D., and Erv Polster, Ph.D., they had the most lasting impact along with the Holy Spirit. Bergantino is the author of "The Essence of Music," "The Art of Psychotherapy and the Liberation of the Therapist," "I Am Freud! Psychoanalysis Is the Only Method of Cure: It's Too Bad No One Knows How to Do One!!!," "Reverse Analysis, the Existential Shift, Gestalt Family Therapy and the Prevention of the Next Holocaust," "Psychotherapy, Insight, and Style: The Existential Moment", and "Making an Impact in Therapy: How Master Clinicians Intervene."

Xlibris Publishing, an Author Solutions, LLC imprint, is a self-publishing services provider created in 1997 by authors, for authors. By focusing on the needs of creative writers and artists and adopting the latest print-on-demand publishing technology and strategies, we provide expert publishing services with direct and personal access to quality publication in hardcover, trade paperback, custom leather-bound and full-color formats. To date, Xlibris has helped to publish more than 60,000 titles. For more information, visit xlibris.com or call 1-888-795-4274 to receive a free publishing guide. Follow us @XlibrisPub on Twitter for the latest news.

###

Dr. Len Bergantino, Ed.D., Ph.D.
THE ESSENCE OF MUSIC
Musicality,
Pure Sound,
The Art of Melody
and Inner Peace
The Essence of Music
Xlibris

The Essence
of Music

Dr. Leo Bergantino, Ed.D., Ph.D.

THE ESSENCE OF MUSIC

Xlibris

This is a book for professional psychotherapists, psychoanalysts, and counselors, students in those areas of specialty; and lay persons who are interested in the essence of effective therapy and how some of the people who do it best practice their art. For professionals, the book presents a personal way of viewing therapy that can add pleasurable options. Each of the therapists with whom I worked, and myself, all had a feeling of enjoyment that we hope will carry over to the office and practices of the readers. For students of therapy, the book offers a search for a professional stature and working posture that may be of value in the development of each student's unique personal style. For lay persons, the book speaks of therapy that can make an impact and speaks of how some of the most potent therapists practice. For Psychoanalysts interested in the work of the Great British Psychoanalyst, Dr. Wilfred R. Bion MRCS (Medical Royal College of Surgeons). This is the only book that demonstrates exactly what he did

I wrote the book with the intention of having it be both an experience and an explanation. I have presented it according to my developmental needs while maturing personally and professionally. This was done so the book might be informative at the conscious level, entertaining at the child level, and persuasive at the unconscious level.

The existential moment is the thread that ties the book together; it is a moment of therapeutic potency. While all moments are existential by definition, there are certain moments that are more powerful in helping patients live happier and healthier lives. Positive results, whether they be from one session or over the long haul, are partially, if not fully, a result of existential moments.

Xlibris

ISBN 978-1-7963-2442-1

Perfect Bound Cover Template

Document Size: 1/2" x 12"

The Art of Psychotherapy and the Liberation of the Therapist   Dr. Len Bergantino, Ed.D., Ph.D.

The Art of Psychotherapy And the Liberation of the Therapist

Much has been written about the Essence of Psychotherapy, but it has remained for Dr. Bergantino to write about the Art of Psychotherapy with such elegant impact.

Dr. Len Bergantino, Ed.D., Ph.D.

8.00 x 8.00

Content Type: Black & White
Paper Type: Creme
Page Count: 540
File Type: InDesign
Request ID: CSS5820069

This is a book for professional psychotherapists, psychoanalysts, and counselors; students in those areas of specialty, and by persons who are interested in the science of effective therapy and how some of the people who do it best practice their art. For professionals, the book presents a personal way of viewing therapy that can add pleasurable options. Each of the therapists with whom I worked, and myself, all had a feeling of enjoyment that we hope will carry over to the office and practice of the student. For students of therapy, the book offers a search for a professional stance and working posture that maybe of value in the development of each student's unique personal style. For lay persons, the book speaks of therapy that can make an impact and speaks of how some of the most potent therapists practice. For Psychoanalysts interested in the work of the Great British Psychoanalyst, Dr. Wilfred R. Bion MRCS (Medical Royal College of Surgeons). This is the only book that demonstrates exactly what he did.

I wrote the book with the intention of having it be both an experience and an explanation. I have presented it according to my developmental needs while maturing personally and professionally. This was done so the book might be informative at the conscious level, entertaining at the child level, and persuasive at the unconscious level.

The existential moment is the thread that ties the book together; it is a moment of therapeutic potency. While all moments are existential by definition, there are certain moments that are more powerful in helping patients live happier and healthier lives. Positive results, whether they be from one session or over the long haul, are partially if not fully a result of existential moments.

Xlibris

The Art of Psychotherapy And the Liberation of the Therapist

Much has been written about the Science of Psychotherapy, but it has remained for Dr. Bergantino to write about the Art of Psychotherapy with such elegant impact.

Dr. Len Bergantino, Ed.D., Ph.D.

THE REVEREND
DR. LEN BERGANTINO, ED. D, PH.D.
The Sanctimonious
Psychoproctological Invasions
THE HANDBOOK FOR POLITICAL ANALYSIS
DR. LEN BERGANTINO, ED. D. (USC), PH.D., D. DIV.
POLITICAL ANALYST
Dorrance Publishing Company

From 2012 through 2018, Len Bergantino began each day with pro bono writings and invasive interventions that insist and expand upon the first amendment rights of United States citizens. In all areas, he is both knowledgeable and feels national, state, and local governments are stuck in socially immobile positions. He created ways to invade entire cultures and governments to move those stuck in quicksand off the dime and into a society that spirals upward. He refers to the creation of these methods as sanctimonious psychoproctological invasions in the creation of a political psychology that should be studies by all human beings who want to make a difference and give meaning to their lives.

About the Author

Len Bergantino is a multi-faceted individual who achieved international prominence in the areas of psychoanalysis, psychotherapy, clinical psychology, and music. His other fields include education and religion, with a precursory knowledge of medicine and law. He is a weathervane in terms of knowing the right thing to do and has the temperament of Che Guevarra in getting it done!

ISBN: 978-1-6461-6218-9 • $xx.xx

SAMPLE

9 780805 995510

ROSEDOG BOOKS
585 Alpha Dr, Pittsburgh, PA 15238

RoseDog Books

The Reverend Dr. Len Bergantino, Ed.D., Ph.D.

From 2012 through 2018, Len Bergantino began each day with pro bono writings and invasive interventions that insist and expand upon the first amendment rights of United States citizens. In all areas, he is both knowledgeable and feels national, state, and local governments are stuck in socially immobile positions. He created ways to invade entire cultures and governments to move those stuck in quicksand off the dime and into a society that spirals upward. He refers to the creation of these methods as sanctimonious psychoproctological invasions in the creation of a political psychology that should be studies by all human beings who want to make a difference and give meaning to their lives.

Sanctimonious Psychoproctological Invasions: The Handbook for Political Analysis

Len Bergantino is a multi-faceted individual who achieved international prominence in the areas of psychoanalysis, psychotherapy, clinical psychology, and music. His other fields include education and religion, with a precursory knowledge of medicine and law. He is a weathervane in terms of knowing the right thing to do and has the temperament of Che Guevarra in getting it done!

The Reverend Dr. Len Bergantino, Ed.D. (USC), Ph.D., D. Div. Political Analyst

To order a copy of
Sanctimonious Psychoproctological Invasions (ISBN 978-1-6461-0238-9)
Email **bookorders@rosedogbooks.com**
or call **1-800-788-7654 (Monday-Friday 9am-4pm)**
The book is also available on Amazon.com and Barnesandnoble.com

WHEN BASEBALL PLAYERS WERE LIKE FAMILY!

My most intense love affair with baseball was between the years 1951 - 1961. Then I went to college and my attentions went elsewhere.

Yet, I returned to baseball by reading baseball books on overseas flights AND NOTICED THAT EVERYTIME I READ ABOUT BASEBALL IT BROUGHT PEACE AND TRANQUILITY TO MY LIFE!

I lived in Waterbury, Connecticut, one hundred miles from New York City and one hundred and eighty miles from Boston. So, after we played baseball all day long (4 or 5 hours) we came in to watch the Yankee game with Mickey Mantle, Yogi Berra, and a pitching staff of Reynolds, Raschi, Lopat and Ford. When they were out of town we watched the New York Giants with Willie Mays, and Sal The Barber Maglie. Then we would blind ourselves at night if we were lucky enough to get WOR Channel 9 by watching The Brooklyn Dodgers, with Carl Erskine, Don Newcombe, Roy Campanella, Gil Hodges, Duke Snyder and Billy Cox. I got to see the Cardinals play Giants and Dodgers so much that I was able to bat left handed out of a crouching position emulating Stan The Man Musial! Musial had such an eye for greatness that the first time he ever saw Pete Rose (Charlie Hustle) run down to first base he said "That kid is going to be in the Hall of Fame Some Day!"

Topps baseball cards were a big item and topic of conversation among the kids. So in a sense major league ballplayers were always in the family conversation in all our homes? What did The Mick do today? What did Berra do today? How did Ted Williams do today? Did the Red Sox win? IT WAS PERSONAL!!!!!!!!!!!!!!!!!!!!!!!!!!!

I loved these guys, even those on other teams. Half of Waterbury were Yankee fans as they won five world series in a row from 1949-1953 and the other half were Red Sox fans because Waterbury's own Jimmy Piersall played right and then center field for the Red Sox and they had the aging Ted Williams, who Mickey Mantle beat out for the batting title in 1956 with an average of .385 while Williams had an average over .400 only he did not have 400 at bats so when they figured it all out Mantle won the triple crown of batting average, runs batted in and home runs. Furthur, the Red Sox had a left handed pitcher named Mel Parnell and every Sunday he threw his glove on the mound he beat the Yankees! I was a Yankee fan so from my point of view he tortured me as I remember listening to every pitch on the radio.

HOW IT ALL STARTED!

We just got a Zenith 12 inch television and my father turned on a baseball game playoff game between The New York Giants and The Brooklyn Dodgers. I was 8 years old. It was the last of the 9th! Some guy named Bobby Thompson, a second stright right fielder, hit a home run off a pretty good Dodger pitcher named Ralph Branca and ruined his life! IT WAS CALLED "THE SHOT HEARD AROUND THE WORLD!"

The Giants played the Yankees and the Yankees won 6 games to 2. The most memorable thing was the Giants second baseman slid into the beloved Yankee shortstop Phil Rizzuto spikes high and ripped his leg open. When they asked Giant Manager Leo Durocher about it his comment was "NICE GUYS FINISH LAST!" The name of the player that slid into the 5 ft. 6 inch Rizzuto was Eddie Stanky.

Stories From Previous Generations

Baseball players who were colorful generated a legacy of stories no matter what generation they were from! Leo Durocher was one of them! I believe his playing career ended before I was born!. I do not hear colorful stories about modern day players!!!!!!!! In my view this diminishes an interest in baseball along with reliable comparable statistics where one could measure a player's accomplishments. For example Bob Feller came up with the Cleveland Indians in 1936. He was an Iowa farm boy who was clocked at throwing 98.6 miles per hour. Only Walter Johnson of the Washington Senators was said to have been faster but there was no means to clock him in 1925. I did see a film clip of him pitching. His arm was so long it hung down to his knees!

Night Games were just coming into existence and the lights were no where as illuminating as today's lights in 2019. Sometime between 1936 and 1939 LEO DUROCHER is facing Bob Feller in one of the first night games. Feller was having trouble with his control. He threw one over the catcher's head. He got two strikes against Durocher and Leo began walking back to the dugout. THE UMPIRE YELLED "HEY LEO, YOU GOT ONE MORE!" LEO YELLED BACK, "CALL ME OUT! I DON'T WANT IT!" 98.6 mph in the dark and Feller just threw one over the catcher's head! Leo was definitely managerial material!

Leo Durocher managed the Dodgers when Jackie Robinson broke the color line in 1947. Leo was carrying on an affair with Hollywood actress

Lorraine Day. Branch Rickey warned him that CYO baseball strongly objected to his infidelity and if he didn't knock it off he would be fired. A time after that when Leo kept on with Lorraine Day whom he later married and then divorced, but at the time introduced Leo to the Hollywood Scene which was a lot of fun! BRACH RICKEY FIRED DUROCHER! THEN HE SAID, "LEO! WAS IT WORTH IT!" LEO RETORTED "YEAH IT WAS WORTH IT!" In other words Leo was not only a bad boy but he wasn't apologizing to anybody for callin em as he sees eml In 1951 when Sports Illustrated usually had a cover picture of some major sport or even fishing; this one issue they had a picture of Lorraine Day in these white shorts! Every 10-12 year old boy athlete would have agreed with Leo that indeed "It was worth it!"

WHO THE HELL WAS LEW BURDETTE!

In the 1990's I realized I had some old baseball cards that may be worth a lot of money. I had Mickey Mantle, Ted Williams, Whitey Ford, Yogi Berra, Robin Roberts and Lew Burdette among them. I brought them to a shop in Westwood and the guy said "You have a few good ones"; but who the hell was Lew Burdette and Robin Roberts? Now, I was a N.Y. Yankee fan and I hated Lew Burdette (so I thought) because he won three games against them when the Milwaukee Braves beat the Yankees in the 1957 world series. I went into a tirade yelling at this guy, "Lew Burdette is that son of a bitch who beat the New York Yankees three games in the 1957 world series and Robin Roberts won 28 games for the 1950 Philadelphia Phillies." The man said, "I am not buying any cards from you! YOU LOVE THOSE GUYS! MOST PEOPLE COME IN HERE AND ALL THEY WANT IS THE MONEY AND THEY HAVE NO IDEA WHO THE BALL PLAYERS WERE OR WHAT THEY DID!" YOU LOVE THOSE GUYS! DON'T SELL THOSE CARDS!!!"

Lew Burdette was a spitball pitcher Yogi Berra said every time he faced Lew Burdette it was like taking a shower. Del Crandall was the catcher for the Milwaukee Braves. He was a great defensive catcher who hit about .220. In an interview he was asked if Lew Burdette used a foreign substance on the ball. Crandall matter of factly answered saying, "No. It was made right here in The United States."

Bob Feller wasn't the sort to give out compliments unnecessarily. When asked about Hank Greenberg, who had 58 home runs in one season, second only to Babe Ruth at the time and was the all time RBI leader Feller merely said, "Hank is afraid of me!

So for Bob Feller to say that THE GREATEST PITCHER HE EVER SAW WAS SATCHEL PAIGE was no small compliment. Satchel Paige pitched in the Negro Leagues when they would not let Black players into the Major Leagues. He threw 100 miles an hour when he was young. I saw him after Jackie Robinson broke The Color Line, pitching for the St. Louis Browns I remember he had a blooper Ball that he threw 15 feet up into the air that batters could not time on the way down. The guy that invented the pitch was Rip Sewell and nobody could time it; that is nobody expect Ted Williams who hit it into the right center field stands some 400 FEET AWAY!

Satch pitched for the Kansas City Monarchs of the Negro League. At 63 years old he was sitting in a wheelchair in the dugout on the cover of a major baseball magazine!

Satch was called up to the Cleveland Indians in 1948 when Lou Boudreau was the manager. Boudreau was a racist from Kentucky and did not want Satch on the team. So Satch had Boudreau hit against him in front of management and Satch did not let Boudrea even get a foul ball. However, when Boudreau put him in a world series game to mop up a lost cause game Satch said he would rather pitch for the Kansas City Monarchs than play for racists like Lou Boudreau.

There were Black players who were better than Jackie Robinson but none who were mentally able to cope with the abuse given to the first Black player in the major leagues. That is why Branch Rickey, general manager of the Brooklyn Dodgers picked Jackie Robinson over Satchel Paige, Josh Gibson, Roy Campanella, Larry Doby and others.

Josh Gibson was a catcher in the Negro League and was said to be the only one to hit a ball some 625 feet out of Yankee Stadium. He played for Pittsburgh.

SATCHEL PAIGE ASKED JOSH GIBSON, "JOSH, WHO IS THE GREATEST OF ALL, YOU OR ME, JOSH?" Paige went on. "Someday, Josh, We are going to square off and find out!" And so it came to pass in the Negro League World Series, Satchel Paige intentionally walked the bases loaded after striking out the first two batters. THEN SATCH MOTIONED FOR ALL HIS OUTFIELDERS AND THEN

HIS INFIELDERS TO SIT DOWN ON THE GRASS, AS HE SAID TO JOSH GIBSON, WHO WAS COMING TO THE PLATE, "LIKE I TOLD YOU JOSH! IT IS COMING DOWN TO YOU AND ME TO SEE WHO IS THE GREATEST OF ALL!" SATCHEL PAIGE STRUCK JOSH GIBSON OUT!

I started watching major league baseball at eight years old in 1951. The color line had already been broken and at eight years old I didn't know anything about it as it was never mentioned on television. I do remember that

1. The Cleveland Indians had Larry Doby, a great hitter as well as Luke Easter at first base -a great clutch hitter!

2. The Chicago White Sox had Minnie Minoso -a colorful outfielder who was always getting the winning hit.

3. The Yankees got Elston Howard around 1956 -a Black catcher who hit over .300 to give Yogi Berra's aging legs a break behind home plate Berra then played left field He was no Gene Wooding in left field.

4. And of course The New York Giants had Willie Mays - the most EXCITING BASEBALL PLAYER I EVER SAW WHO INTRODUCED THE BUSHEL BASKET CATCH.

5. Home Run Derby was a television show with a White announcer in a cordial manner having Mickey Mantle square off against Willie Mays and Hank Aaron. I got to see a rerun of this show some fifty years later, and Mays and Aaron looked like they were afraid of getting lynched! THERE WAS A LONG DISTANCE BETWEEN WHAT WAS POLITICALLY CORRECT THEN AND WHAT IS POLITICALLY CORRECT IN 2019.

6. The New York Giants also had a third baseman named Monte Irvin who was one helluva baseball player - hitter and fielder! Any of these players might have been chosen for their outstanding play in the Negro League instead of Jackie Robinson but they could not have held up with the mental stress of being the first to break the color barrier. Jackie Robinson gave his life to do so. He died at a very early age and looked like an old man long before his time!

7. The Dodgers also had a pitcher named Don Newcombe who won 27 games for them around 1955 and he hit 7 home runs. Of all

the Dodgers he hit the most vicious line drives!!! He pitched right handed and batted left handed.

WHEN BASEBALL WAS KING THE NEW YORK YANKEES WERE KING OF BASEBALL AND GEORGE HERMANN RUTH (BABE RUTH WAS THE SULTAN OF SWAT

Many say the 1927 Yankees were the greatest team of all time. They had murderers row with a lineup of Tony Lazzeri, Bob Muesel, Lou Gehrig and Babe Ruth.

While Roger Maris, Sammy Sosa, Mark McGuire and Barry Bonds all hit more than 60 home runs as well as Hank Aaron none will ever take the place of Babe Ruth as "THE KING OF BASEBALL". Babe wore a King's crown, a big fur coat and drove a Stutz Bearcat convertible (perhaps the most stylish car of it's day).

One day Babe Ruth was in Al Capone's Nightclub in Chicago where Capone was not only the Capo Di Tutti Di Capo but had several people murdered. Ruth went up to his table and asked Capone's girlfriend to dance. Ruth told Frank Nitti (his underboss) that "If it were anybody but Babe Ruth I would have him whacked!" Capone then called Babe Ruth over to his table and said "Hey Babe! I hear you made more money than the President last year!" Ruth retorted "I had a better year than the President!" (Ruth it 60 home runs that year in 1927.)

THE NEW YORK YANKEES WERE WORLD CHAMPIONS FOR FIVE STRAIGHT YEARS FROM 1949-1953.

They had Mickey Mantle taking over from Joe DiMaggio in center field; Yogi Berra catching; Frank Crosetti as third base coach; Bill Dickey as first base coach and mentor to Berra as a defensive catcher; Joe Collins at first baae replaced by Moose Skowron, Bobby Richardson at 2nd base; Phil Rizzuto at shortstop replaced by Tony Kubek; Gil McDougald at third base; Gene Woodling in left fiel and Hank Bauer in right field. The most knowledgeable relief pitcher I ever saw was Johnny Sain who used to start for the 1948 Boston Brave along with Warren Spahn. Their motto was "Spahn and Sain and pray for RAIN!" Spahn would up with 363 career wins, only behind Cy Young who had 511 career wins! When the Yankees brought Sain in rarely did anyone do anything against him. He just knew more about pitching than anyone I had seen at the time until I saw Maddux pitch a game for the Dodgers around 2006!

Greg Maddux won 353 games in his career, only behind Warren Spahn at 363, Roger Clemens at 354 and Cy Young himself who won 511 games I SAW CY YOUNG THROW OUT THE OPENING PITCH AT A NEW YORK YANKEES OLD TIMERS GAME WHEN HE WAS EIGHTY SEVEN YEARS OLD! IT WAS A THRILL CY YOUNG PITCHED FOR THE CLEVELAND INDIANS! JACK CHESBRO <u>WON 42 GAMES FOR THE NEW YORK YANKEES ONE YEAR!</u> <u>(9 inning games)</u>

The New York Yankees had Billy Martin playing second base. Mantle, Whitey Ford and Billy Martin went out on the town one night and a fan started an argument and one of the Yankees had to take the fall and it couldn't be Mantle or Whitey Ford, a great Yankee pitcher So George Weiss, a prick in his own right, blamed Billy Martin for the incident and traded him to Kansas City. The Yankees had a great pitching staff of Allie Reynolds, Vic Raschi, Whitey Ford and Eddie Lopat - who had eight speeds and breaks to his curve ball. Casey Stengel was the manager and George Weiss told Stengel, when any of these goes get close to 20 wins in a season, don't pitch them any more. I DON'T WANT TO GIVE THEM A RAISE! AS THEY WON FIVE STRAIGHT WORLD CHAMPIONSHIPS HE ALSO KEPT ALL BUT WHITEY FORD OUT OF THE HALL OF FAME! THEY DID NOT HAVE ENOUGH WINS TO QUALIFY THANKS TO WEISS!

Allie Reynolds was Stengel's go to guy. He pitched two no hitters in 1951! He and Bob Feller were my two pitching idols. Reynolds I got to see pitch a lot and emulate and Bob Feller wrote a great book entitled <u>HOW TO PITCH!</u> FELLER ACTUALLY PITCHED FOR THE INDIANS BETWEEN HIS JUNIOR AND SENIOR YEAR OF HIGH SCHOOL WHEN HE WAS SEVENTEEN YEARS OLD AND THEN RETURNED TO HIGH SCHOOL HIS SENIOR YEAR TO GRADUATE! HE HAD THREE NO HITTERS AND ELEVEN ONE HITTERS IN NINE INNING GAMES!!!

GREAT MANAGERS

Perhaps the greatest manager was John McGraw of the New York Giants in 1923. Casey Stengel played for McGraw and was a great student of John McGraw's managerial skills. On the other hand the Yankees were so good and Casey was such an old man-close to seventy - that the players just let Casey go to sleep during games on the bench; and would occasionally wake him when they felt it was a critical decision that went beyond their own self management skills.

THE KIDS LIVED AND DIED WITH EVERY PITCH IN ROUTING FOR THEIR OWN TEAMS!. AS I WAS A DIEHARD YANKEE FAN I SAW A WORLD SERIES GAME IN SEPTEMBER, 1953 THAT WAS THE MOST DOMINANT GAME I EVER SAW ANYONE PITCH. THE BOOKLYN DODGERS WERE PLAYING THE NEW YORK YANKEES AND CARL ERSKINE WAS PITCHING! HE STRUCK OUT FOURTEEN YANKEES, INCLUDING MICKEY MANTLE FOUR TIME IN THROWING A TWO HITTER! EVERY STRIKEOUT WAS LIKE HAVING A NAIL BANGED INTO YOUR COFFIN, ONLY YOU COULD STILL FEEL THE HAMMER AND THE NAIL! Somewhere when Vin Scully was still the Dodger announcer I Chastised him for never mentioning Erskine's performance (OISK IS WHAT THE BROOKLYN CROWD CALLED HIM) Vin Scully sent me back an autographed letter and then I called Erskine and told him about it. He was a bank vice-president or president somewhere in his home state of Indiana. He sent me a copy of his book -I think it was called Dodger Blue and he loved Mantle as did those from other teams such as Denny McClain -the last 30 game winner who pitched for the Detroit Tigers in 1967. Erskine said he was 89 years old. He said "I guess I threw a little harder that day! Our backs were to the wall!" Then he said "There is a picture in the book of Mickey Mantle and he signed it "To The Greatest Pitcher I Ever Faced!" Just the feeling I had about Erskine was that The Dodgers ought to be bringing him out for Spring training every year to TRAIN PITCHERS HOW TO GIVE IT 110% IN WINNING THE BIG ONE!. I WAS TEN YEARS OLD WHEN ERSKINE PITCHED THAT GAME! I WAS IN AWE!

Dr. Len Bergantino – Educational Consultant

Doctor of Education – University of Southern California
M.A in Education – Fairfield University – Jesuit Trained (424) 293-9511

Joe Palladino, (Sports Director - Waterbury Republican-American) THIS LETTER IS TO BE SENT TO EACH OF THE MEMBERS OF THE COMMITTEE REGARDING THE BUILDING OF A STATUTE OF JIMMY PIERSALL IN HAMILTON PARK!!! (It will be published in my next book which will be dedicated to Major League Baseball from 1951-1961. Let's Begin:

JIMMY PIERSALL WAS MAJOR LEAGUE BASEBALL IN WATERBURY, CONNECTICUT FROM 1947 until I loved to California in 1968. HE WAS GOOD TO THE KIDS AND HE WAS GOOD TO THE CITY.

Jimmy Piersall was one of three Waterburians that were famous. The other two here Rosalind Russell and George Metesky (The Mad Bomber).

In 1955 (Summer) Rosalind Russell was going to have the premiere of one of her movies in Waterbury instead of Graumann's Chinese in Hollywood. That night, a flood put Waterbury about twelve feet under water; and the Waterbury Republican had a front page story (paraphrased) "BLACK ROSALIND BRINGS FLOOD TO WATERBURY!" She was so insulted that she never came back to visit her mother publicly again. Rosalind made the mistake of trying to put a city on the map who already thought it was on the map!

George Metesky, who Rod Steiger played in the movies, used to make Timex watches for 30 years. At the end of his thirty they gave him a timex and forced him to retire. And so he became The Mad Bomber in New York City!

Both Rosalind Russell and George Metesky felt that Waterbury shortchanged them in terms of their lifetime efforts! Let's NOT MAKE THE SAME MISTAKE WITH JIMMY PIERSALL!!!

I SAW PIERSALL PLAY MANY TIMES! HE WAS THE GREATEST DEFENSIVE OUTFIELDER OF HIS DAY, AND PERHAPS ANY OTHER DAY! FURTHUR, HE WAS THE MOST COLORFUL BASEBALL PLAYER OF ANY DAY!

IF YOU WERE FROM WATERBURY AND YOU LOVED MAJOR LEAGUE BASEBALL, YOU TALKED ABOUT THE NEW YORK YANKEES (FIVE TIME WORLD CHAMPIONS), MICKEY MANTLE, YOGI BERRA (who only struck out 13 times in one full season), Ted Williams, the fourth place Boston Red Sox (4 out of 8), and Jimmy Piersall!

I played in the JIMMY PIERSALL LEAGUE on a team that won the championship three years in a row, and Jimmy Piersall threw all the kids a banquet of hot dogs, baked beans and coca colas. He had former Waterbury Sports writer Dan Parker as the guest speak. As he then wrote for the New York Times he came in especially for Piersall! Piersall had friends in high places!

Then Piersall had each of us walk through a line and he shook hands and said a few words to each of us! WE LOVED JIMMY PIERSALL AND I WAS A DIEHARD YANKEE FAN!!!

Another thing Piersall did for Waterbury is bring major league baseball players to Municipal Stadium in Waterbury, (I remember either 1953 and 1954 or 52-53). He had Yogi Berra and Yankee pitcher Vic Raschi on the one I remember most. In both of those games Piersall was playing right field and made magnificent leaping catches to rob two hitters of home runs!

PIERSALL AS WAS SAID RAN LIKE A DEER! IN OTHER WORDS HIS LEGS MOVED DIFFERENTLY THAN OTHER MAJOR LEAGUE PLAYERS THEY MOVED LATERALLY! I SAW HIM ROB YOGI BERRA ON AT LEAST THREE OCCASIONS ON MAGNIFICENT LEAPS OVER THE 297 foot WALL IN YANKEE STADIUM WHEN THE BALL WAS ALREADY WELL INTO THE CROWD!

PIERSALL GAVE TICKETS TO THE ENTIRE TEAM TO GO TO FENWAY PARK IN BOSTON AFTER WE WON THE PIERSALL

LEAGUE CHAMPIONSHIP! WE LOVED JIMMY PIERSALL! HE WAS GOOD TO THE KIDS!

HAMILTON PARK WAS ALWAYS THE MOST SPECIAL PLACE TO PLAY YOUTH BASEBALL! IT HAD TWO LARGE DIAMONDS! AND AS PIERSALL WAS AN EAST ENDER FROM WATERBURY IT IS ONLY FITTING THAT HIS STATUE BE IN HAMILTON PARK!

LET'S HOPE WATERBURY HAS LEARNED FROM THE HISTORY OF IT'S MISTAKES WITH ROSALIND RUSSELL AND GEORGE METESKY AND NOT SHORTCHANGE PIERSALL OR GIVE ONE OF HIS MANY CHILDREN THE OPPORTUNITY TO SUE THE CITY FOR AGE DISCRIMINATION! I AM SURE ALL THE PLAYERS BEFORE 1970 FEEL THIS WAY AND THAT INCLUDES PROFESSIONAL BASKETBALL AS WELL AS PROFESSIONAL FOOTBALL!

Cordially,
Dr. Len Bergantino

Formerly baseball coach and Park Department Supervisor at City Mills Lane and Catholic elementary school baseball coach and public grammar school umpire.

Players and Managers

Casey Stengel was said to have talked to players and managed the Yankees in a language that was all his own that baseball players referred to as "SCHIZOPHRENESE" BILLY MARTIN WAS THE ONLY ONE CAPABLE OF LEARNING AND MANAGING IN THIS "STENGELESE" MODALITY AND HE WAS THE ONLY ONE THAT BECAME A GREAT YANKEE MANAGER, HIRED TWICE AND FIRED THREE TIMES BY THE BOMBASTIC GEORGE STEINBRENNER OF THE NEW YORK YANKEES (OWNER FROM CLEVELAND). IT WAS SAID THAT EVERY TIME REGGIE JACKSON STRUCK OUT GEORGE STEINBRENNER WOULD MAKE AN EYE DOCTOR APPOINTMENT FOR HIM!.

ROBIN ROBERTS PITCHER 1950 Philadelphia Phillies Whiz Kids

Robin Roberts won 28 games for the 1950 Philadelphia Phillies. He was known to give up a lot of gopher balls -home runs. The Yankees bought him in the fifties and they were doing him dirt. He was a lot better than they gave him the opportunity to show! The Yankees traded him to The Baltimore Orioles. It was one of the few times I rooted against the Yankees as an old Robin Roberts pitched a masterpiece against them and whipped their Yankee asses! Even then I liked old people who were getting screwd.

Allie Reynolds -NY Yankee Pitcher from 1950-1953

In 1949 Casey Stengel asked one of the immortals Joe DiMaggio, who he should get as an additional pitcher for the Yankees. Dimaggio said "Why don't you get Allie Reynolds from the Cleveland Indians! I can't hit him!" This was the Joe DiMaggio that hit in 56 straight games in 1941.

Reynolds pitched two no-hitters in 1951 and when he hit Roy Campanella on the right index thumb in the first game of the 1953 World Series vs. the brooklyn Dodgers Stengel said, "Allie just won the world series for us!" Another way to look at it is that Stengel gave full credit to just how good Roy Campanella was as both a catcher and a hitter. Reynolds last year was 1953 due to a severe back injury from an automobile accident and Campanella became confied to a wheelchair after an automobile accident. The Dodgers always had Campanella at Spring Training to coach the Dodgers.

Charlie (Chuck) Dressen was a Dodger Manager who lost the 1952 or 1953 world series to the Yankees. As far as I could tell he was an excellent manager and I didn't understand why he got fired?

<u>Walter Alston -Dodger Manager from 1954 through the 1970's</u>

Walter Alston was a big guy and he was pretty much in the background so there were not many stories about him; but there was one! Alston was on the team bus and the Dodgers were laughing, having a godd time after getting their asses beat. Alston stopped the bus and threatened to kick the living shit out of any Dodger who thought it was funny to lose! After that I understood why they hired him.

Taking A Sick Day May Cost More Than It Is Worth!

In 1923 the New York Yankees had a very good first baseman named Wally Pipp. He took a sick day and Lou Gehrig replaced him. That is, HE REPLACED HIM FOR THE NEXT 2154 straight games! I never got to see Gehrig play but the best first baseman and hitter I ever saw was GIL HODGES OF THE BROOKLYN DODGERS. I think he hit about .314.

He commanded such respect that Dodger rookie pitcher Don Drysdale used to call him "Mr. Hodges". Drysdale was pitching in his first all-star game and Ted Williams was coming to bat. Drysdale called time out and walked over to first base saying "Mr. Hodges. How should I pitch to Mr. Williams?" Hodges said, "Throw him low and away curve ball". Drysdale put it exactly where Hodges told him to and Williams hit a line shot home run into the left field stands. Drysdale went over to Hodges and said "Mr. Hodges, I put the ball exactly where you told me to and Mr. Williams hit it for an opposite field home run!. Hodges daid, "SON! HE WOULD HAVE HIT ANYTHING YOU THREW HIM! I JUST DIDN'T WANT HIM HITTING IT AT ME!"

<u>TED WILLIAMS IN HIS LAST FEW YEARS!</u>

I was at Fenway Park in Boston. Ted Williams came up to take batting practice! The entire ballpark stopped talking! You could't hear a pin drop! Ted Williams hit about twenty of the hardest hit balls (vicious line drives) that I have ever seen in my life. He hit them so hard off the wall they almost bounced back to second base! No wonder Hodges didn't want Williams hitting the ball at him! All I had to see was Williams take batting practice and even as an old man about to retire, **I KNEW I HAD SEEN THE GREATEST HITTER THAT EVER LIVED!** Furthur, he was the last and may be the last player to ever hit .400!

In 1941 Williams approached the final day of the season hitting .400 and his manager asked him if he wanted to sit the last game out so as not to blow the batting title. Williams said backing into a title is no way to win it, and at the end of that game he had four more hits and a .406 batting average!

THE NEW YORK YANKEES WERE NUTS!!!

1. In 1951 they hated Mantle for taking DiMaggio's place. They only came to love Mantle when Roger Maris got there!
2. The Yankees did not want Roger Maris to break Babe Rith's record of 60 home runs in one season. There is a psychoanalytic phenomena called severe pathological projective identification mostly understood by the British Psychoanalytic and Melanie Klein's folle. That phenomena involves one or more persons being able to project their own madness and hatred into another person as they did to Roger Maris, who lost all his hair on the way to his 61st home run! He couldn't wait to get traded to the St. Louis Cardinals!

The Yankees Had Won About 27 World Series Through 1964

THE ST. LOUIS CARDINALS PLAYED THEM ABOUT SIX TIMES AND BEAT THE YANKEES FOUR OUT OF SIX WORLD SERIES AND I THINK 1964 MADE IT FIVE This statistic used to piss me off to no end, the realization that The St. Louis Cardinals, with only a few stars such as Stan The Man Musial, had a better organization than the New York Yankees!

Enos (Country) Slaughter -St Louis Cardinal Right Fielder was known for his hustling - a Pete Rose before Pete Rose! As goes the way of all talented elders, The Yankees bout him! He won the "Comeback of The Year Award! Slaughter said, "Comeback of the Year Award, HELL! I NEVER WENT AWAY!"

CARL FURILLO, BROOKLYN DODGER RIGHT FIELDER, HAD THE BEST ARM I HAVE EVER SEEN IN AN OUTFIELDER! IN THREE STRAIGHT GAMES I SAW HOTTERS GET SINGLES TO RIGHT FIELD AND FURILLO THROW THEM OUT AT FIRST BASE!

YOGI BERRA -YANKEES CATCHER has over 300 career home runs and only struck out 13 times in one entire season. yogi was a hot shit

He had been thrown out of a game by Lester Shylack in a late season game for cussing at the umpire. It was a gruelling hot double header at Fenway after the pennant was already decided and Berra wanted to get thrown out so he yelled at Shlack exactly what he said before and Lester said "Berra, if I've got to stay out here in this heat, so do you! No shut up and play ball!"

Casey Stengel - Glendale's Most Famous Citizen (CA) or "BottleArse" as he was called by some Red Sox Fans, When Stengel walked to the mound you could see him from behind and he was shaped like a coke bottle!

ALLIE REYNOLDS - the great Yankee Pitcher -#22 -my first idol! I got to see him on television being interviewed during the time Bud Wilkinson, coach of The Oklahoma Sooners had about 49 straight victories. The announcer asked Allie Reynolds what the difference was playing for the Cleveland Indians and The New York Yankees. He was a Cherokee Indian. Reynolds said "In Cleveland they called me COPPERHEAD AND OLD BLANKETASS. IN NEW YORK THEY CALL ME THE SUPER CHIEF! THAT IS THE DIFFERENCE! I WAS SHOCKED BECAUSE AT THE TIME HE SAID IT NO ONE SAID ANYTHING LIKE THAT ON TELEVISION!

MEL ALLEN - The Yankees television and radio announcer gave Reynolds the name The super Chief. He was always smoking White Owl Cigars and drinking Ballantine Ale on the show as this was not prohibited in those days.

MAN FOR MAN THE DODGERS WERE BETTER THAN THE FIVE TIME WORLD CHAMPION NEW YORK YANKEES BUT THEY COULD NEVER BEAT THEM IN THE WORLD SERIES. Let's compare lineups:

First Base Yankees -Joe Collins Dodgers -Gil Hodges -.314 Average

2nd base -Billy Martin -12 hits in 1953 world series vs. Junior Gilliam -Excellent average and excellent fielder

3rd base Gil McDougall -adequate fielder -over .300 batting average. Billy Cox - hit around .220 but best fielding 3rd baseman I have seen in my lifetime.

Shortstop Pee Wee Reese -over .300 batting average -adequate fielder - Yankees Phil Rizzuto -over the hill.

Catcher -Yogi Berra -Hall of Famer vs. Roy Campanella who Case Stemgel said "Allie Reynolds just won the world series for us when he hit Roy Campanella on his right thumb. IN OTHER WORDS, STENGEL THOUGHT CAMPANELLA WAS THAT GOOD Yogi hit his home runs over the 297 foot short right field fence. Campanella mostly hit smashes over the left center field wall.

Pitchers: The Yankees had Reynolds, Raschi, Lopat and ford. The Dodgers had Carl Erskine, Clem Labine (average), Preacher Roe (somewhat mesmerizing), and later Don Newcombe.

Perhaps the Yankees success the Dodgers can be attributed to the events that begin the 1955 World series. Alston said, "Who wants the ball?" meaning who wanted to pitch the first game Even though Don Newcombe had won 27 games that year he refused when a spunky kid named Johnny Podres said "I can beat the Yankees every day of the week and twice on Sunday!" Podres won three games for Alston who had faith in the kid! and the Dodgers won the 1955 world series!

Right Field - Carl Furillo -right field -.306 batting average; the greatest throwing arm in the history of baseball vs. Yankees Hank Bauer -also a .300 hitter - adequate fielder - United States Marine and the toughest son of a bitch on the team!

Center Field -Mickey Mantle - one of the three greatest long ball hitters in the history of baseball -the other two being Babe Ruth and Josh Gibson. Duke Snyder -great outfielder and great home run hitter. In any other city except New York he would have been the primary attraction, but Snyder was unlucky in that Mantle played center field for the Yankees and Willie Mays played center field for the New York Giants!

Left Field -Gene Woodling -.314 hitter -left handed batter -great outfielder -Dodgers in 1955 had Sandy Amoros who robbed Berra of a home run in a spectalular catch!

The Yankees traded Woodling to the Baltimore Orioles in return for Don Larsen, Bob Turley who was better than Don Larsen, and Willie Miranda a great fielding no hitting shortstop.

THE ONLY WORLD SERIES GAME I EVER MISSED!

I never went to school during world series time! Except for one game -the game Don Larsen pitched a perfect game for the Yankees! I didn't think Don Larsen was that good! BUT HE WAS THAT DAY! I remember getting home from school, turning on the television and seeing Dale Mitchell swing at strike three and Yogi Berra Running out to the mound and jumping into Don Larsen's arms with Mel Allen yelling "DON LARSEN HAS JUST PITCHED THE FIRST PERFECT GAME IN WORLD SERIES HISTORY"! THAT WAS 1956! Who knew it was going to be the last perfect game in world series history!

THE ONLY FIGHT I EVER HAD WITH MY TRUMPET TEACHER

Carl Berg played for Harry James. I never missed a lesson in six years. He was from Pittsburgh. We bet double or nothing on a trumpet lesson! Bill Mazeroski hit a home run in the ninth inning and Pittsburgh won the 1960 world series! I was pissed! Diehard Yankee Fans were nuts back then and I was one of them! I remember Yankee shortstop Tony Kubek got hit in the Adam's apple with a ball that took a bad hop and the Pirates got good pitching performances out of Bob Friend, Vernon Law, and Fork Ball pitcher Elroy Face!

DUTCH LEONARD WAS A KNUCKLEBALL PITCHER FOR THE 7th out of 8 place Chicago Cubs. I loved watching him pitch. Later you had Hoyt Wilhelm, Phil Neikro and catcher Clint Courtney for the old St. Louis Browns having a catcher's mitt made the size of a pizza.

DON DRYSDALE was one of the two great Dodger pitchers during the Koufax era (1957-1963). He was sick after a Met's game and had to stay back in New York. Someone said to him, "Hey, I hear your buddy Koufax pitched a one hitter today!" Drysdale said, "Yeah, but did he win!" The Dodgers notoriously did not score many runs in those days, usually 1 or 2.

Drysale was a huge fellow, about 6 ft. 4 inches and about 240 pounds. He was slow off the mound on a bunt. It was a world series game against the Yankees. Mickey Mantle bunted and his foot hit first base just before Drysdale. Drysdale ran his foot on top of Mantle's as hard as he could while twisting his cleat into Mantle's foot and he said, "I make my money pitching. You make your money hitting home runs. I don't care if you hit a home run off of me, BUT DON'T EVER DO THAT AGAIN! Mantle, five foot eleven inches tall and 185 pounds said "Don't Worry! I Won't!"

RICHIE ASHBURN was the slight of built two time batting champion of the 1950 Philadelphia Whiz Kids. In a game against the New York Giants at a time when most hitters never hit more than 2 or 3 foul balls in one at bat I SAW RICHIE ASHBURN HIT 17 FOUL BALLS IN A

ROW I think it was in 1953 or 1954. As I was 11 years old than I remember being bored out of my mind waiting for the game to continuing RATHER THAN REALIZING THAT WAS THE GAME!

CURT SIMMONS AND ROBIN ROBERTS WERE THE TWO BEST PITCHERS ON THE WHIZ KIDS UNTIL CURT SIMMONS WAS FORCED TO RETIRE BECAUSE HE CUT HIS TOES OFF WITH A POWER LAWN MOWER! I thought, what a waste!

HARVEY HADDIX, THE LITTLE KITTEN, PITCHED FOR THE ST. LOUIS CARDINALS AND THE PITTSBURGH PIRATES AND ONE DAY PITCHED A TWELVE INNING NO HITTER AND LOST THE GAME 1-0!

HOME RUN BAKER HAD THE HOME RUN RECORD AT 12 BEFORE BABE RUTH HIT 53 in 1923 and 60 in 1927. IMAGINE GOING FROM TWELVE TO FIFTY THREE! THE FANS MUST HAVE GONE ABSOLUTELY WILD WHEN BABE RUTH HIT THE SCENE. RUTH ALSO HAD MOST SCORELESS INNINGS AS A LEFT HANDED PITCHER IN A WORLD SERIES in 1916 UNTIL WHITEY FORD BROKE HIS RECORD WITH 29 scoreless innings!!!

THE YANKEES HAD WHITEY FORD PITCHING AND THE GIANTS HAD WHITEY LOCKMAN PLAYING FIRST BASE! Imagine calling somebody Whitey in today's political climate!

One of my old coach's attended a golf tournament with Mickey Mantle somewhere between 1971 and 1973. I had asked him to sign my business card "to Dr. Len Bergantino - The GREATEST PITCHER I EVER FACED." He said Mantle didn't want to do it at first saying that Whitey Ford and Sandy Koufax would be pissed at him!" However he did sign it exactly that way. Also of note Mantle was looking out the window of a high rise in New York and nostalgesically said "I USED TO OWN THIS CITY!" So much for retirement?

Bobby Shantz- a pitcher for the Philadelphia Athletics -five feet six inches and slender - baffled the hitters so the Yankees bought him!

JOHNNY MIZE, THE BIG CAT, PLAYED FORST BASE FOR THE ST. LOUIS CARDINALS IN HIS YOUTH! HE WAS A GREAT PRESSURE HITTER SO THE YANKEES BOUGHT HIM AS A PINCH HITTER AND MORE TIMES THAN NOT HE DIVERED IN THE CLUTCH!!!

October 15, 2019

THE REASONS THE DODGERS WILL NOT WIN THE WORLD SERIES NEXT YEAR!!!

1. The Dodgers are cheap in that they will not pay for what they need to win. Two examples are they passed up in the bidding for Max Scherzer and Justin Verlander.

2. THE DODGERS FILL THE STANDS WITHOUT WINNING A WORLD SERIES!!!

3. THE DODGERS RELY ON THE FACT THEY WON 106 GAMES AS A REASON TO CONTINUE TO MISLEAD THE PUBLIC THAT ALL IS WELL!

4. THE DODGERS ARE ENABLERS FROM TOP TO BOTTOM SO IT IS DIFFICULT TO KNOW IF PEOPLE ARE BEING FORCED INTO LESS OPTMMAL DECISIONS.

5. For example, while Clayton Kershaw has proven over time that he is one of the best pitchers in the history of baseball HE HAS ALSO PROVEN HE CANNOT PITCH WITH ANY DEGREE OF CONSISTENCY IN THE PLAYOFFS. WITH THESE FACTS DAVE ROBERTS MIGHT DECIDE TO KEEP KERSHAW ON THE ROSTER AND GRATEFULLY ACCEPT HIS SIXTEEN REGULAR SEASON WINS WITHOUT EVER PLACING HIM ON THE PLAYOFF ROSTER FOR THE DURATION OF HIS TENURE WITH THE DODGERS! ANYTHING ELSE IS THE MANAGER BEING AN ENABLER BY PLAYING THE PROTECTION GAME TO NOT HURT SOMEONE OF KERSHAW'S STATURE.

6. Unless these organizational corrections are made THE DODGERS ARE AN ORGANIZATION THAT IS BOTH TOO CHEAP TO WIN IT ALL, AND ARE GUILTY OF PLAYING THE PROTECTION GAME WHICH IS AT THE ROOT OF ALL PSYCHOSES WHICH RENDERS THEM INCAPABLE OF WINNING THE WORLD SERIES NEXT YEAR.

7. Unless Sports editors are willing to publish the nitty gritty THE DODGER'S COMPLACENCY MIGHT LEAVE THEM WINNING 107 GAMES WITHOUT WINNING THE WORLD SERIES NEXT YEAR!

Sincerely,

Dr. Len Bergantino - Dodger Fan since 1968 (formerly Supt. of Instruction)
P.S. On two occasions 3 Star General Howard Graves, then Supt. of Instruction at West Point, invited me to train cadets in authority and leadership!
cc: President "Donald Trump"

You Need At Least Two Great Pitchers And Two Good Ones To Win A World Series

The Yankees had Reynolds And Ford (Great) and Raschi & Lopat (Good). The Cleveland Indians from 1953-1955 had the greatest pitching staff ever assembled. In 1954 they won 11 games with Bob Feller (great), Bob Lemon (20 game winner), Early Wynn (over 300 lifetime wins) and Mike Garcia who won 16! In 1955 they added Don Mossi and Ray Narleski to the bullpen. They were both great In 1955 the Indians brought up a left handed flame thrower named Herb Score! Yankee third baseman Gil McDougall hit a line drive back to the pitcher's box that hit Herb Score right in the eye. He lost his eye and had to quit baseball, so we never got to find out what he could become! McDougall had a conscience and felt he could no longer play baseball as he knew he could not emotionally tolerate any kind of repeat of the Herb Score incident. McDougall, as I remember, was always hitting around .312.

BATTING AVERAGES THEN AND NOW

Batting averages were higher from 1951-1961 than they are now. Perhaps it has to do with starters going only 7 innings, and the number of 100 mile an hour or at least 98 mile an hour one inning relievers of today's game. Most of the players on good teams were batting over .300. Today you see a lot of .250 hitters with television announcers complimenting them for their excellent .250 hitting. Ted William .406 does not seem in Jeopardy by any stretch of the imagination.

BILLY PIERCE, VIRGIL TRUCKS AND SUNDAY DOUBLEHEADERS Chicho White Sox had two great pitchers. I was a diehard Yankee Fan and either Billy Pierce or Virgil Trucks would always beat the Yankees in one game of the doubleheader. One of Cleveland's big four also would beat the Yankees one out of two in Sunday doubleheaders! The Red Sox only had lefty Mel Parnel but he beat them every time he pitched on Sunday!

THE ANTIDOTE TO THE GREATEST PITCHING STAFF IN HISTORY OF THE 1954 Cleveland Indians was WILLIE MAYS AND THE 1954 New York Giants who beat the Indians Four Straight! No one in the country saw that one coming. The Giant won the Division with about 92 wins.

THEY DID HAVE SAL (THE BARBER) MAGLI WHO THREW SO CLOSE TO BATTER'S HEADS BEFORE HELMETS THAT THEY USED TO CALL HIS PITCHES CHIN MUSIC OR SAY SAL THE BARKER GAVE HIM A SHAVE TODAY!

RADIO AND TELEVISION ANNOUNCERS OF TODAY PLUS PETE ROSE

After the playoffs they have a good time talking to each other remembering the good old days when they used to play. Pete Rose was different and by far the best television announcer I have ever seen. PETE ROSE KNOWS AND CAN EDUCATED THE GENERAL PUBLIC ON THE DETAILS OF BASEBALL AS ONLY A GREAT INSIDER MIGHT KNOW! BUT PETE ROSE GOT FIRED AGAIN FOR SOMETHING HE DID FOUR HUNDRED YEARS AGO! AND SO IT IS I AM BORED TO TEARS WITHOUT HIM!

MARK MCGUIRE

was a class act who hit 70 home runs, breaking Roger Maris's record of 61 home runs set in 1961. Mrs. Maris and their children attended the event and McGuire was so gracious it seemed to be A REGAL EVENT.

BARRY BONDS

I saw him it his 600th home run and a few others into McCovey Cove (which was something to see in it's own right-that is, boats with ores in the water waiting for Bonds to hit one to them). He hit 73 home runs in a single season and 743 lifetime. San Francisco loved him. HE HAD THE FASTEST WRIST ACTION I HAD SEEN SINCE TED WILLIAMS. HANK AARON AND ERNIE BANKS WERE NEXT!

ROGER CLEMENS

I loved watching Roger Clemens pitch. I was sixty years old and I used to tell my son "When I grow up I want to be like Roger Clemens. At the time I was already an internationally renown clinical psychologist and musician) One day I walked in and my son said "He Dad, ROGER CLEMENS IS GOING TO JAIL!) (354 career wins)

CONGRESSMAN HENRY WAXMAN

Congressman Waxman and I became cordial via many psychopolitical written interventions into the Senatorial/Congressional Cesspool of politics. Waxman was very bright and had a law degree from UCLA. Although I did my doctoral work at The University of Southern California (SC) Waxman and I had a mutual respect and liking for each other. The one exception was the day he asked Mark McGuire about steriod use and McGuire said he "didn't like to talk about history." That kept McGuire and Sammy Sosa out of the hall of fame as well as Bonds and Clemens! Along with Pete Rose they all belong there! They are among the greatest of all time! ??? Waxman know my views ???

October 11, 2019

Dave Roberts - Manager - Los Angeles Dodgers

When Carl Whitaker, M.D. trained me he always brought things back to what he referred to as THE EXISTENTIAL FACTS OF THE SITUATION:

1. As an organization THE DODGERS DON'T CHUCK UP ENOUGH TO MAKE THE GAME WORK:
2. You had a chance to get both Scherzer and Verlander which would have made the rest of my letter unnecessary.
3. You have won 7 division titles without a World Series victory!
4. You are delusional when it comes to Kershaw! The existential facts are that a) He won 16 games during the year; b) After back surgery he never had the pinpoint accuracy he had prior to surgery. YOU AND THE DODGERS REFUSE TO ACCEPT THIS! REMEMBER, IN BASEBALL "YOU ARE AS GOOD AS YOUR LAST AT BAT!"
5. KERSHAW IS UNLUCKY! HE HAS GIVEN YOU AND THE DODGERS THESE EXISTENTIAL FACTS IN SEVERAL (PLAY OFFS AND) WORLD SERIES WHERE HE CANNOT GET IT DONE AS HE WOULD HAVE DURING THE REGULAR SEASON! I HEARD YOUR RECENT AFTER ELIMINATION SPEECH THAT YOU FEEL COMFORTABLE WITH THAT WHICH MEANS YOU WILL MAKE THE SAME MISTAKE OVER AND OVER! KERSHAW'S DAY IS OVER! BUEHLER IS YOUR BEST PITCHER NOW!

Sincerely,

Dr. Len Bergantino
cc: Kershaw and Sports Desks
Dodger Fan Since 1968.

BECOMING A DODGER FAN DRYSDALE VS. BOB GIBSON -St. Louis Cardinals. I moved to Los Angeles in 1968 to pursue my doctoral work at The University of Southern California. Bob Gobson, who was as strong as a horse without any pitching finesse that interested me was pitching vs. Don Drysdale in a contest of most scoreless innings pitched consecutively. I forget who won. The number of innings was in the sixties, although I am going from memory alone in writing this book, so while my stats might be off a bit, the feeling of the times is accurately portrayed. Dodger Stadium was alive with excitement! IT WAS A BIG EVENT! I LOVED GOING TO THE BIG EVENT! PERHAPS THAT IS WHY I CAN STILL REMEMBER A LOT OF THEM IN WRITING THIS BOOK!

Mickey Mantle had 16 world series home runs in a time before playoffs existed.

Billy Martin, scrawny, Yankee second baseman, had 12 hits in a 7 game world series in 1953!

Carl Erskine pitched the most dominant game I ever saw. In the 1953 world series, when the Yankees were at their peak, Erskine blew away 14 of them as if they didn't exist! He struck out Mantle four times! I know I am writing this twice but Erskine deserves it! At the time Mantle wrote "To The Greatest Pitcher I Ever Faced" "Carl Erskine". I called Erskine some fifty years later and told him. He was a Bank President in Indiana! He said, "Perhaps I threw a little harder than usual that day!" He loved Mantle and was so proud about what Mantle wrote to him in an autographed picture! He sent me a copy of his book DODGER BLUE with Mantle's autographed picture!

It bothers me that the great players of my era are all but forgotten. I hate to see great athletes that I loved and provided me with untold entertainment forgotten as if they never existed even if they play for opposing teams and I did not know a great deal personally about them. There were only 16 teams then, eight in the American League and eight in the national league. The American League usually won when they squared off! Some of the players I remember:

1. Ralph Kiner -1951-most home runs-Pittsburgh Pirates -37 home runs -married to Nancy Chaffee - all pro tennis player!
2. Al Kaline -Detroit Tigers right fielder - came up when he was 19 years old and made the all star team every year!

3. Harvey Kuenn-Detroit Tigers shortstop -man year she got 200 hits.

4. Denny McLain -Tigers Pitcher-1967-last 30 game winner!!!

5. Jackie Jensen-boston Red sox outfielder -quit at the top of his game when major leagues expanded. REFUSED TO FLY IN AIRPLANES!

6. Wald Dropo - Red sox first baseman from Mooseup, Connecticut. Even Dropo didn't know where Moose up Connecticut was!

7. Dom DiMaggio played center field for Red Sox. Joe played center field for the Yankees and a third brother played for the Pittsburgh Pirates but did not last as long as Joe and Dom.

8. WILLIE MAYS MADE THE MOST SPECTACULAR CATCH I EVER SAW IN THE 1954 WORLD SERIES WHEN VIC WERTZ, FIRST BASEMAN FOR THE CLEVELAND INDIANS HIT IT ABOUT SEVEN MILES OVER HIS HEAD AND MAYS RAN BACK AND MADE ONE OF HIS FAMOUS BUSHEL BARREL CATCHES!!! INCIDENTALLY, HE WAS BARRY BONDS GODFATHER! BONDS SURPASSED WILLY MAYS 600+ home runs! I saw his father Bobby Bonds when he played for the Waterbury Giants around 1967 when the Waterbury Giants were a farm club os the San Francisco Giants. Vic Raschi -came to Waterbury around 1953 or 1954 with the Jimmy Piersall All Stars and I was excited to see him pitch. Then a little kid ran out when Raschi was walking to the dugout and asked him for his autograph. RASCHI PUSHED HIM TO THE GROUND! YEARS LATER I FOUND OUT RASCHI USED TO PSYKE HIMSELF UP WITH ANGER TO PITCH. HOWEVER, I NEVER COULD STOMACH TO SEE HIM PITCH AGAIN AND I WAS GLAD THE YANKEES TRADED HIM TO THE ST. LOUIS CARDINALS BEFORE HE EVER THREW ANOTHER PITCH FOR THE YANKEES! APPARENTLY HE WAS FINISHED AS HE HAD ONE OR TWO MEDIOCRE YEARS AND THAT WAS THAT!

9. Tony Kubek, Yankee shortstop, got hit with a bad hop ground ball right in the Adams apple. It put him out of the 1960 world series.

10. Jose Altuve -Houston Astros - 2019 - could have started off for any major league team in any era! A magnificent baseball played who comes through in the clutch! (It seems like every time!

11. Jason Verlander would have been one of the best pitchers in the game in any era! A strong heat throwing right hander who doesn't throw too many snake balls - today known as a slider that bounces in the dirt and make hitters look stupid swinging at it. I don't like looking at it even if it works!

WHAT DO PHIL RIZZUTO AND JOSE ALTUVE HAVE IN COMMON?

THEY WERE AND ARE FIVE FOOT SIX INCHES TALL!

Rizzuto was the best bunter I ever saw!

Other than long ball home run hitter Mickey Mantle Jose Altuve is one of the best cluth home run hitters I ever saw! And he is only five ft. 6 inches tall! Imagine if he were 5 ft. 7 in. tall!

FERNANDO MANIA - FERNANDO VALENZUELA!!!!!!!!!!!!!!!

1981 Fernando was not as good as Whitey Ford but he had a better level of concentration, getting himself in and out of jams with men on base - CREATING AN ELECTRICITY THAT COULD HAVE GOTTEN HIM ELECTED AS THE FIRST MEXICAN AMERICAN MAYOR OF LOS ANGELES IF HE WANTED THE JOB! Fernando sealed the deal on my emotional transfer from being a New York Yankee Fan to becoming a Los Angeles Dodger Fan!

MANNY RAMIREZ AND MANNYVILLE
(LEFT CENTER FFIELD)

When Manny Ramirez got traded from the Red Sox to the Dodgers he lit Los Angeles on fire in a way I had only experienced with Fernando Valenzuela! WHAT EXCITEMENT! IT FELT LIKE MANNY COULD GET A HIT OR WIN A GAME ANY TIME HE CAME TO BAT! YOU HAD TO BE THERE TO BELIEVE IT! Later they claimed he used steroids. Can you see why I didn't give a shit if McGuire, Sosa, Bonds, or Clemens used steroids! They were the closest thing to the kind of entertainment provided by the 1949-1953 five time world series champion New York Yankees! The Houston Astros are the closest thing to that state of ecstacy in 2019! I am writing this a day before the world series starts against The Washington Nationals!

Alex Kellner, a left handed pitcher for the last place CLINT COURTNEY -ST. LOUIS BROWNS & BALTIMORE ORIOLES CATCHER WHO HAD A CATCHER'S MITT MADE THE SIZE OF A LARGE PIZZA TO CATCH THE KNUCKLEBALL

WITHOUT BREAKING HIS HANDS! THERE WERE A LOT OF COLORFUL BASEBALL PLAYERS THAT BROUGHT FANS TO THE TURNSTILES! CLINT COURTNEY WAS ONE OF THEM!

HOYT WILHELM -BALTIMORE ORIOLES KNUCKLEBALL PITCHER PITCHED UNTIL HE WAS FORTY FIVE YEARS OLD! Clint Courtney got traded from the St. Louis Browns to the Baltimore Orioles to catch Hoyt Wilhelm!

George Brett - Kansas city Royals - a great hitter. One year he was hitting .400 late in the year. He would up around .353. Harmon Killebrew of the Minnesota Twins was a huge man who was a great home run hitter!

Ferris Fain was a golden glove left handed first baseman in the early 1950's who was a decent hitter, around .300. Bob Porterfield was a hard throwing right hander that occasionally beat the Yankees while pitching for the fifth place Washington Senators.

Bill Veeck was general manager of the St. Louis Browns and one year he had a midget playing right field. There was also a one arm outfielder. Veeck would do anything to sell tickets! As the Browns were always in last place he was a Godsend! Luis Aparicio was the Chicago White Sox shortstop in the early fifties! He was a cut above the rest in the plays he made! Minnie Minoso was a great outfielder and cluth hitter for an early fifties Chicago White Sox team!

Luke Easter was a monster in size for The Cleveland Indians at first base. His clutch extremely hard hitting helped beat the Yankees on many occasions. He was Black.

Larry Doby was Black. He was a home run threat every time he came to bat! As a diehard Yankee Fan I was afraid of both Luke Easter and Larry Doby. I wished they never came to bat! So Jackie Robinson integrated baseball in 1947, about six years before the ten year old me was into baseball, so as far as I knew blacks were playing major league baseball and when I played growing up they were both good guys and good teammates, usually a cut above the average baseball player, what I never realized until I was much older is that there was a very subtle pressure that Blacks had to be a notch above the average to get in! TAKE ELSTON HOWARD - The New York Yankees catcher hired so they could rest Yogi Berra's aging legs while keeping his bat in the lineup as a left fielder. Yogi was a clutch hitter and he had that 297 foot right field fence down in his sleep! ELSTON HOWARD COULD DO EVERYTHING WELL -catch - hit -field! THE FIRST TWO PROFESSIONAL BASEBALL TEAMS WERE

THE BALTIMORE ORIOLES AND THE CINCINNATI REDLEGS (AROUND 1868.

RABBIT MARANVILLE WAS THE STAR SHORTSTOP FOR THE CONCINNATI REDLEGS AROUND 1868.

I mention this because when I did my doctoral work at the University of Southern California in EDUCATION (COUNSELOR EDUCATION) they informed me that what I had to agree to was A TRANSMISSION OF THE CULTURE, SO THAT OTHERS WOULD KNOW WHAT TRANSPIRED, PRIOR TO THEIR ERA! AT THE TIME USC HAD ONE OF THE FOUR TOP SCHOOLS OF EDUCATION IN THE UNITED STATES; the others being Harvard, Columbia (Teachers College) and Stanford Universities.

THAT WAS BEFORE THE GULAGS TOOK OVER!

CHUCK STOBBS was a left handed pitcher for the Washington Senators in the early 1950's who beat the Yankees enough that they tried to buy him. The deal fell through! The Yankees didn't generally lose world series. they bought up everybody and anybody who could beat them! AS MEL BROOKS SAID IN HIS MOVIE HISTORY OF THE WORLD PART I "IT IS GOOD TO BE KING!" SPEC SHEA WON 13 games for the 1947 Yankees. He was from the next town over, Naugatuck Connecticut! He was a little on the chunky side and he was from Naugatuck, Connecticut, 7 miles down the road from Waterbury, Connecticut, my home town! When I was a junior in high school I had a date with the Captain of the Naugatuck cheerleaders, Barbara Joan Sheedy, who was one of the most attractive young ladies in the Naugatuck Valley. My father said, "What's a matter! You couldn't find anybody in town!?" In those days nobody ever left Waterbury. They lived in the same house for 50 years. They had the same job for forty years!

JOE PAGE WAS A TOP RELIEF PITCHER, LEFT HANDED, IN 1949. He got arm trouble so I didn't get to see him.

ALEX KELLNER WAS A LEFTY WHO COULD BEAT THE YANKEES PITCHING FOR THE LAST PLACE PHILADELPHIA ATHLETICS WHICH LATER BECAME THE LAST PLACE KANSAS CITY ATHLETICS.

CONNIE MACH BOTH OWNED AND MANAGED THE PHILADELPHIA ATHLETICS. IF MY MEMORY SERVES ME HE DID SO FROM ABOUT 1915 to the middle 1950's! I didn't know much about him other than the other owners loved him! They used to call him "The Grand Old Man of Baseball!"

The 1957 Milwaukee Braves that beat the Yankees in 7 games in the World Series had a few good hitters:

Eddie Matthews played third base He wound up with over 500 home runs.

Hank Aaron wound up breaking Babe Ruth's 714 lifetime home run record.

Joe Adcock was a good model for me in that he was a right handed first baseman who could hit.

Billy Bruton was a great fielding center fielder who couldn't hit in an era where Mickey Mantle, Willy Mays, and Duke Snyder played center field and hit a lot of home runs!

MOOSE SKOWRON, A COLLEGE FOOTBALL PLAYER FROM PURDUE, TOOK OVER FOR JOE COLLINS AS YANKEE FIRST BASEMAN! MOOSE HIT A LOT OF DOUBLES, MANY HOME RUNS AND CONTRARY TO JOE COLLINS DID NOT PUT ME TO SLEEP!

THE NEW YORK GIANTS HAD ALVIN DARK WHO MOVED FROM SHORTSTOP TO SHORTSTOP-MANAGER TO MANAGER! HE WAS SMART AND HE WAS EXCELLENT -NOT GREAT!

ELROY FACE (FORKBALL PITCHER), BOB FRIEND, AND VERNON LAW WERE GOOD ENOUGH FOR THE PITTSBURGH PIRATES IN 1960 TO BEAT THE NEW YORK YANKEES IN THE WORLD SERIES. THE THING THAT AMAZED ME was that just a few years before the PIRATES WERE IN LAST PLACE! Johnny Vandermeer is the only pitcher (left handed) in the history of baseball to throw consecutive no-hitters. He did it for the Cincinnati Reds in 1939!

LITTTLE KLU - Ted kluzewski _FIRST BASEMAN FOR THE CINCINNATI REDS in the mid fifties had 18 inch arms and he used to wear his shirt cut up on the sleeve to showcase those eighteen inch arms. All the boys in the neighborhood were in awe. He was a good hitter and won the equivalent of the golden glove award several years. He hardly moved off of one spot but at that spot nobody could hit anything by him! They called him "Little Klu" because he was the smallest of his three brothers! This blew peoples' minds ROY MC MILLAN -shortstop for the Cincinnati Reds in the mid fifties was an excellent shortstop who lasted many years!

THE SCREWBALL - a pitch thrown by a leftie that would break left or thrown by a rightie that would break right was first developed cy a great pitcher Christy Matthewson in 1905 and called THE FADEAWAY! Matthewson lasted until he was gassed in WWI!

FERNANDO VALENZUELA WAS THE BEST SCREWBALL PITCHER I EVER SAW IN MY LIFETIME! FURTHUR, HE WAS THE TOUGHEST PITCHER I HAD SEEN SINCE WHITEY FORD IN TERMS OF WORKING HIMSELF IN AND OUT OF TROUBLE WITH MEN ON BASE!!! FORD HAD 29 scoreless innings for the Yankees in the world series. That broke Babe Ruth's 1916 record. EWELL BLACKWELL -THE WHIP -RIGHTHAND MASTER OF THE SIDEARM PITCH - HE THROWS FROM THIRD BASE! Cincinnati Reds -late forties! I never saw him pitch until the Yankees bought him in the mid-fifties and by that time he had lost "The Eye of The Tiger".

Dee Fondy was a left handed first basemen for the Chicago Cubs and later the Pittsburgh Pirates. Occasionally he parked one in the stands against the Dodgers.

HAPPY FELTON'S KNOT HOLE GANG. Happy Felton was an overweight good natured guy that had a 15 minute pre game show before Brooklyn Dodger Games that began with a little kid looking through a knot hole in a wooden fence because he didn't have money to pay for a ticket. The first time I went to Yankee Stadium I sat right behind the screen behind home plate and Yogi Berra was right in front of me. THE PRICE WAS $1.25 per ticket! No wonder they called baseball THE GREAT AMERICAN PASTIME! Happy Felton had regulars from the Brooklyn Dodgers teaching kids one baseball skill per day! I LOVED THAT SHOW AND MADE A POINT OF VIEWING IT EVERY TIME I COULD! I LEARNED A GREAT DEAL FROM SOME GREAT PLAYERS!

CATCHERS - The New York Giants had Wes Westrumand Smokey Burgess played for more than one team!

2019 Pitchers I like watching are Walker Buehler -Dodgers, Jason DeGrom and sondegaard of The Mets and to some degree Gerrit Cole -Houston Astros and Max Scherzer of the Washington Nationals.

THE SNAKE BALL - As a joke a pitcher used to throw a ground ball to his catcher and call it a snakeball. TODAY PITCHERS REGULARLY THROW PITCHES THAT BOUNCE IN THE DIRT BEFORE THEY GET TO HOME PLATE OR JUST AS THEY GET TO HOME PLATE. THEY ARE CALLED SLIDERS AND HITTERS OFTEN SWING AT THEM LOOKING FOOLISH! I LIKE WALKER BUEHLER THE BEST BECAUSE HE DOESN'T THROW SNAKE BALLS! HE JUST BLOWS IT BY THEM AT 99 miles an hour!

I have done my best via recall from 60 years ago to give HONORABLE MENTION TO ALL THOSE MAJOR LEAGUERS THAT WERE "GOOD ENOUGH TO BE REMEMBERED!"

I HOPE YOU HAVE AS MUCH FUN READING MY MAJOR LEAGUE BASEBALL RECOLLECTIONS AS I HAD LIVING THEM!

October 23, 2019

Mark Lombardo
Chairman
Bureau of Parks
185 South Main Street, first Floor
Waterbury, Conn. 06706

Dear Mark Lombardo,

RE: NOMINATIONS FOR THE HANK O'DONNELL HALL OF FAME FOR NEXT YEAR -JIMMY PIERSALL STATUE

Dear Mark Lombardo,

I am sending a nomination for next year as I am 76 years old and at that age cannot count on being around to send it next year.

Jimmy Piersall was baseball in Waterbury! Furthur he was the most entertaining baseball player of all times and the greats loved him! Mantle, Berra, Williams!

Sincerely,

Dr. Len Bergantino
Park Dept. Supervisor
City Mills Lane -1963

Former Teacher -Wilby High School
Former grammar school baseball coach and umpire
Former Freshman basketball coach at Wilby -undefeated. Had I stayed in Waterbury, Jack Delaney was grooming me to become head basketball coach at Wilby much as he did with Gilmore at Sacred Heart.

October 26, 2019

Andrew Friedman   & Dave Roberts

General Manager   Manager   **LOS ANGELES DODGERS**

Dodger Stadium

RE: FRIEDMAN DISCUSSING KENLEY JANSEN AFTER ELIMINATION ON TV

1. Kenley Jansen and Clayton Kershaw are the two most mentally disciplined pitchers in the major leagues. Their performance is different, however their mental discipline remains par excellence.
2. The problem both pitchers have is that their bodies will not perform as they did prior to Kershaw's disc surgery and Jansen's chronic atrial fibbrillation. **THIS IS BORNE OUT BY THE EVIDENCE!**
3. It totally amazes me they can do what they are currently doing albeit it is a long way from what they were able to do! **THIS IS ONLY BECAUSE OF BEING THE TWO MOST MENTALLY DISCIPLINED PITCHERS IN THE MAJOR LEAGUES THAT THEY ARE ABLE TO DO WHAT THEY ARE CURRENTLY DOING!**
4. Thus your idea of giving them a good talking to when they have a mental discipline that far exceeds anyone I have seen other than Ted Williams, Barry Bonds, Hank Aaron, Roger Clemens, et. al. is ridiculous as a substitute in that they cannot physically perform at the levels they once did and those are the existential facts of the situation!

Sincerely,

Dr. Len Bergantino
cc: Jansenn & Kershaw
P.S. 1 It is a felony to intercept or withhold federal mail!

cc: Ned Colletti
on outside of letter:
"It is a felony to withhold Federal Mail!"

<u>DECLARATION OF THE REVEREND DR. LEN BERGANTINO</u>

I, The Reverend Dr. Len Bergantino, declare: Prior to April 9, 2015 I sent a letter to both the Los Angeles Dodgers and Carl Erskine stating that Carl Erskine pitched the most dominant game I ever saw pitched in the 1953 world series when he struck out 14 New York Yankees, including Mickey Mantle four time. I received a letter dated April 9, 2015 from Carl Erskine that said: "Hello Dr. Len - Naturally you make my day with your letter and comments about Oct 2, 1953. Yes I was motivated that day for failing in game one of that series. - Campanella was my catcher and he caught numerous great pitchers including I believe Satchel Paige - Canoy said it was the greatest game he ever caught. Of course he hit the game winning home run off of Rashi - Here's my latest book - Hope you enjoy it. - Carl Erskine #17 Retired President* Star Financial Bank He also wrote "To Dr. Len Bergantino, In appreciation for being at my best game and your devotion to education and baseball. (see page 148) Sincerely, Carl Erskine #17 "Oisk" 4/9/15 page 148 is a picture Mickey ??? Mantle gave "To Carl The Greatest W.S. (world series) ??? Pitcher in the world Mickey Mantle 4 K's (K=strikeouts) I declare under penalty of perjury that the foregoing is true and correct and I would and could testify as such in a court of law if called upon to do so. Dec. 1 written in Los Angeles CA 12/18/19

Dr. Len Bergantino

A Note From *Carl Erskine*

April 9, 2015

Hello Dr. Len —

Naturally you make my day with your letter and comments about Oct 2, 1953. Yes I was motivated that day for failing in game one of that series. — Campanella was my catcher and he caught numerous great pitchers including I believe Satchel Paige — Campy said it was the greatest game he ever caught. — Of course he hit the game winning home run off of Raschi. — Here's my latest book — Hope you enjoy it. —

Carl Erskine #17

41
TALES FROM THE
DODGERS
DUGOUT

March 28, 2015

Carl Erskine
Pronounced "Oiskine" by Brooklyn Dodger Fans
c/o Los Angeles Dodgers
Dodger Stadium
1000 Elysian Park Avenue
Los Angeles, CA 90090

Dear Carl Erskine,

I am writing this letter to you and sending it to the media in that I think history has shortchanged you IN THAT I HAVE STUDIED GREAT PITCHERS AND YOU PITCHED THE MOST DOMINANT BASEBALL GAME I HAVE EVER SEEN PITCHED AGAINST THE NEW YORK YANKEE TEAM THAT WON FIVE WORLD SERIES IN A ROW AND HAD A LINEUP WHERE PRACTICALLY EVERYONE BATTED OVER .300 WHEN MICKEY MANTLE AND YOGI BERRA WERE IN THEIR PRIME! Thus, I urge you to get a VHS of the World Series Game in 1952 or 1953 in which you pitched a two hitter and struck out 14 New York Yankees, including Mickey Mantle four times and have this tape played at least once every six months on the Dodger Television station.

How I happen to remember the game so well is that I was a die hard New York Yankee fan at the time and you tortured me for nine innings worse than other great pitchers who had success against the Yankees. These included Early Wynn, Bob Feller, Bob Lemon and Mike Garcia of the Cleveland Indians; Billy Pierce and Virgil Trucks - one of which always beat the Yankees in Sunday double headers for the Chicago White Sox; Mel Parnell of the Boston Red Sox who beat them five times a year; Sal Maglie of the New York Giants; Don Newcombe the year he won 27 games, et. al.

As I recall the Yankee lineup Mantle was over .300, Berra was about .308, Gene Woodling was .314, Hank Bauer was .306, Gil McDougald was .312, Rizzuto was always a threat with the bunt, Joe Collins was over .300.

You pitched the most dominant game including Don Larsen's perfect game, many no hitters, Whitey Ford's 27 win season, as well as later greats such as Nolan Ryan, Don Drysdale, Roger Clemens, et. al. You had a directly overhand fastball that I have never seen since you in quite that way. You were not that big physically.

It is my sincere hope that this letter will help bring you the notice that you deserve in your twilight years. I also wrote it because I am one of the few old enough to remember the game!

With The Greatest of Respect and Admiration,
Dr. Len Bergantino - Los Angeles Dodger Fan

April 15, 2015

Dear Carl Erskine (Oisk),

Thank you for a copy of your book, your letter, your writing inside the book, and drawing my attention to page 148, where Mickey Mantle gave you an autographed pitcher saying you were "the greatest pitcher in the world". (acknowledging you struck him out four times).

I would say from 1952 through 1954 I saw all the home games of the New York Yankees and New York Giants on Channel 11 (WPIX) all the Dodger home games at night on channel 9 (WOR TV).

Mel Allen was the voice of the Yankees and he often said amidst a cloud of smoke (White Owl Cigars) and a broadcasting buzz (Ballantine Ale) that the New York Yankees from 1949-1953 were either the greatest team in baseball history or the second greatest, behind the 1927 Yankees.

Now it wasn't just that you beat them and you struck out fourteen of them, setting a world series record while you struck out Mantle four times; the reason I said you pitched the most dominant game I ever saw pitched IS YOU MADE EITHER THE GREATEST OR SECOND GREATEST TEAM IN THE HISTORY OF BASEBALL LOOK LIKE THEY DIDN'T EXIST! LIKE NOBODY WAS HOME!

From Your writing it looks like Mantle and Roy Campanella agreed with me. The reason I wrote you about the games I saw is that Roy Campanella was the greatest hitting catcher I ever saw. He had this undefinable quality that when the game was on the line you just knew he was going to beat you! You mentioned he hit the home run off of Vic Raschi that won the game for you!

Casey Stengel knew how good he was. When Allie Reynolds hit Campanella on the right index finger in game 1 and it swelled up Stengel said "Reynolds just won the world series for us!"

Mel Allen asked Allie Reynolds what the difference was between pitching for the New York Yankees and the Cleveland Indians. Reynolds was a Cherokee Indian from Oklahoma. He said "In Cleveland they used to call me Copperhead and Old Blanket Ass. In New York they call me The Super Chief. That's the difference!"

I love baseball stories and I can't wait to read your book "Tales From The Dodgers Dugout" by Sports Publishing, NY, NY. ©200???

When I See You In My Mind's Eye, I See You As You Were Then!

Once Awesome, Always Awesome!

Dr. Len Bergantino

April 20, 2015

Dear Carl Erskine (#17),

A story for Jimmy. It was 1972 and I was flying from San Diego to Los Angeles when a pushy fellow told me to move over a seat and let him sit next to me, that it was going to be the most unusual flight of my life. I said "Why is that?" He said, "Because I am an M.D.!" I said, "What's so unusual about that?" He said, "Look at my fingers. I have web fingers, and I have Downs Syndrome." "I am the only M.D. you will meet in your lifetime who has Down's syndrome. I am a researcher who was called in from Hawaii to Scripps Institute of Oceanography to do research on marine biology."

Also enclosed is an article I wrote some 12 years ago about Al Hir

Warm Personal Regards,
Len Bergantino

For Publication

April 20, 2015

UNSOLICITED BOOK REVIEW OF "TALES FROM THE DODGERS DUGOUT" WRITTEN BY CARL ERSKINE AND PUBLISHED IN 2004 by SPORTS PUBLISHING which is a Division of Skyhorse Publishing, Inc. A Delaware Corporation. 233 pp.

Around 1992 I went to a Sports memorabilia shop in Westwood, CA and attempted to sell some of my childhood baseball cards. I had one of Mickey Mantle that was worth $1200 at the time. I also had cards of Robin Roberts and Lew Burdette whom I respected but gave me grief in that they regularly beat teams I favored. The storeowner had no idea who they were. I began to argue that Robin Roberts won 28 games in 1950 and Lew Burdette beat the New York Yankees 3 times in the 1957 World Series!

Then the storeowner said, "You love these guys! Don't sell the cards! Most people who come in here just want the money and they don't even know who the players are! You love these guys! Don't sell the cards! Keep them always!" I was stunned and I thanked him and I turned around and walked out!

Carl Erskine has written this kind of book! You will love these guys! Many times the book brought tears to my eyes!

Mickey Mantle was offered a $5000 check when he came up in 1950 and he said "Imagine, they pay me for this too!" Carl Erskine wrote the entire book with that depth of boyhood feeling he never lost of the joy of being a big league pitcher while bringing the humanity of many into the forefont.

I am 71 years old. Ted Williams was the best hitter I ever saw! Stan Musial was right up there! Mickey Mantle made us all wonder every time he came to bat whether he would hit one out of Yankee stadium! Willie Mays was the most exciting ballplayer I EVER SAW! Carl Erskine pitched the most dominant game I ever saw pitched. If he only won one game in his entire career and that was it, the game he struck out 14 Yankees and Mickey Mantle four times in the 1953 World Series, I WOULD STILL SAY IT WAS THE MOST DOMINANT GAME I EVER SAW ANYONE PITCH BECAUSE HE MADE A TEAM THAT WAS BEING COMPARED WITH THE 1927 YANKEES AS

THE GREATEST TEAM IN BASEBALL HISTORY LOOK LIKE NOBODY WAS HOME! LIKE THEY DIDN'T EXIST! Nobody ever did that to <u>those Yankees!</u>

What puzzles me is that sports writers hardly ever mention many of the greatest baseball players of all time and treat them as if they did not exist! CARL ERSKINE'S BOOK BRINGS MANY OF THESE BASEBALL GREATS FROM ALL TEAMS TO THE FOREFRONT BOTH IN TERMS OF BASEBALL SKILLS AND THEIR HUMANITY AND GOOD WORKS IN THE WORLD AT LARGE! THIS BOOK IS A MUST READ!

Written by Dr. Len Bergantino

May 2, 2015

Dear Carl Erskine,

The copy of your book that you sent me, TALES FROM THE DODGERS DUGOUT, evoked a flood of memories about the era in which you pitched for the Brooklyn Dodgers. I feel it is a lost era and there is practically no way to explain the level of excellence and the emotion that accompanied NEW YORK CITY BASEBALL. IMAGINE, THE BROOKLYN DODGERS, NEW YORK YANKEES AND NEW YORK GIANTS ON CHANNEL ELEVEN AND NINE EVERY DAY AND NIGHT!

For example, Mickey Mantle, Willie Mays and Duke Synder all playing center field in the same city; along with Roy Campanella and Yogi Berra as catchers! Pitching the Dodgers had Carl Erskine, Preacher Roe; the Giants had Sal Maglie and Johhny Antonelli and the Yankees had Reynolds, Raschi, Lopat and Ford. The best fielding third baseman I ever saw was Billy Cox. The Dodgers also had a right fielder with the best arm I ever saw, Carl Furillo, who I saw several times throw out a runner on a base hit would be single at first base from right field, and gun down runners at home plate like he threw from the mound!

Me and all my 12 year old baseball cohorts watched about 200 games a year of all three New York teams and Happy Felton's Knox Hole Gang was our all time favorite show in that major leagurer's would actually give us kids tips on how to play baseball. My favorite shows were you on pitching, Gil Hodges on how to play first base and Carl Furillo.

When baseball was King, New York was King of baseball and YOU WERE A BIG PART OF IT. All the kids had your baseball cards, and most had the cards of all the players on each team and knew their batting averages and won-lost pitching records.

Today hardly anyone is on the same team long enough to fall in love with them. It is hard to explain why we loved you guys, whether you were on our favorite team or you beat us, YOU MADE OUR LIVES A LOT BETTER THAN THEY WOULD HAVE BEEN.

FOR EXAMPLE, ONE THING I REMEMBER ABOUT WILLIE MAYS WAS THAT HE MADE A DOCUMENTARY "THE SAY HEY KID" WHERE IN 1954 HE WAS PLAYING STICKBALL WITH

ALL THE LITTLE BLACK KIDS IN THE POORER SECTIONS OF NEW YORK

THANK YOU AGAIN FOR YOUR BOOK, FOR BEING CARL ERSKINE, AND FOR GIVING US KIDS A LIFETIME LEGACY THAT NO SPORTS TODAY CONVEY IN TERMS OF A TRANSMISSION OF THE CULTURE!

WITH AFFECTION,
Dr. Len Bergantino

May 19, 2015

Dear Carl Erskine,

I do things my unconscious mind tells me to do when there is unfinished business and so I write this letter.

From what I wrote to you you might think I idealized you and your era of baseball. Actually YOU AND YOUR FELLOW BASEBALL PLAYERS WERE SO DIFFERENT THAT WE PLAYED BASEBALL FROM SUN - UP 9 a.m. to sundown at 9 p.m. You had that affect on us!. Even the worst of us dreamed of playing in The Big Leagues some day! And we worked tirelessly and were pretty good kids along the way. There were no gangs. There were no drive by shootings. There were no drugs and we all had the idea if we wanted to play major league baseball we probably should not smoke or drink.

Baseball made us feel safe in growing up as Americans! and the more we knew about it, the better!

I used to pitch and play first base so my favorite Dodgers were you and Gil Hodges! I was in awe of Carl Furillo's throwing ability from right field!

I am cutting out new turf in creating a proactive field of political psychology intended to effect societal change and the unfinished business I had in writing this letter was to ask you if you have any ideas I might try to implement to bring America's youth back to simpler times! If you want credit for the ideas I will credit you. If you prefer to remain anonymous I will merely attempt to implement your ideas as best I can.

Cordially,
Dr. Len Bergantino

From the Vatican, 17 June 2019

Dear Mr Bergantino,

His Holiness Pope Francis has received your letter, and he has asked me to thank you.

The Holy Father will remember you in his prayers, and he invokes upon you God's blessings of joy and peace.

Yours sincerely,

Monsignor Paolo Borgia
Assessor

____

Mr Len Bergantino
1215 Brockton Avenue
Suite 104
Los Angeles, CA 90025
USA

FIVE OTHER BOOKS I HAVE WRITTEN SINCE 1981 FOUR OF WHICH WERE PUBLISHED BY XLIBRIS PUBLISHING COMPANY IN 2018-2019 AND THE LAST PUBLISHED IN 2019

*** THE MINIMUM CONDITIONS REQUIRED TO ACHIEVE THE COMPLETE DEVELOPMENT OF YOUR OWN BEING REQUIRES THAT YOU READ EACH OF THE BOOKS IN A MANNER WHERE THE WORK IS INTEGRATED AT A DEEP AND SUBSTANTIVE LEVEL. THE BASEBALL BOOK ROUNDS OUT THE CHILDHOOD FUN ASPECTS OF YOUR PERSONAL DEVELOPMENT.

November 21, 2019

Dear Psychoanalyst,

I want you to be on the lookout for a book recently sent by my publisher entitled I AM FREUD! PSYCHOANALYSIS IS THE ONLY METHOD OF CURE! IT'S TOO BAD NO ONE KNOWS HOW TO DO ONE!!!

THIS BOOK AND OTHERS I HAVE WRITTEN WILL HELP PSYCHOANALYSTS BECOME "HIGHER SENSITIVES" (as written about in a book in 1967 by Shaffica Karagulla, DeVorss Press). This will make all the difference in successfully working through transferences.

My first book, PSYCHOTHERAPY, INSIGHT AND STYLE: THE EXISTENTIAL MOMENT, 1981 Allyn & Bacon, 1994 retitled MAKING AN IMPACT IN THERAPY: HOW MASTER CLINICIANS INTERVENE, Jason Aronson, Inc. is an important preface in that the psychoanalytic chapter actually has interviews with the best of Wilfred Bion's Analysands-Supervising and Training Analysts - M.D.'s as well as the order in which Bion's books must be read to develop the level of attention required for psychoanalysis to, in "good faith" continue to grow as a profession! Analysts thought Bion's work was brilliant conceptually and theoretically but not relevant to the practice of psychoanalysis. THIS IS NOT TRUE AND I AM FREUD, THE BOOK IT TOOK ME FORTY YEARS TO WRITE, DEMONSTRATES MANY OF HIS UNIQUE TECHNICAL APPROACHES TIED TO THE QUALITY OF BEING OF THE PSYCHOANALYST.

FURTHUR, BION SAID "THE ENTIRE PSYCHOANALYTIC LIBRARY IS GOOD for about the first hour and one half of an Analysis! After that YOU HAVE TO KNOW WHAT TO SAY TO THE PATIENT!" Martin Grotjahn, MD told me "Psychoanalysis is a great method of education, but it is ineffective as a method of treatment!"

My also new book "The Art of Psychotherapy And The Liberation of The Therapist" remedies both the concerns of Bion and Gortjahn! As I was trained by 17 or more world renown psychiatrists, psychoanalysts and clinical psychologists THIS UPDATED VERSION OF FORTY YEARS OF THE EXISTENTIAL MOMENT PROVIDES BOTH OPTIONS OF WHAT YOU SAY TO A PATIENT THAT MUST BE INCORPORATED INTO PSYCHOANALYTIC EDUCATION IN WAYS THAT PROVIDE EFFECTIVE TREATMENT! LOOK

AT IT THIS WAY! FOR $300,000 OVER A 7 YEAR PERIOD OF FIVE DAY A WEEK ANALYSIS THE PATIENT HAS A RIGHT TO COME OUT OF THE ANALYSIS NOT AS CRAZY AS THE DAY THEY WENT IN!

Sincerely,

Dr. Len Bergantino, Ed.D. (USC), Ph.D.A.B.P.P.

P.S. I AM THE ONLY ONE WHO COULD ACTUALLY DO ALL OF WHAT WILFRED BION WROTE!

Do you think that some slug who looks very professional who "<u>whispers</u>" an occasional interpretation to you five times a week for 7 years can make one bit of difference in your life or does such a psychotoxic slug called a psychoanalyst merely stick you in an emotional toilet bowl for seven years having the cumulative result of turning you into a hopeless bastard who will never turn the tragic corner in his or her life?

Can your analyst analyze an archaic liquid symbiotic or an osmotic transference, or can they even recognize this phenomena in order to analyze it? If the psychoanalyst cannot analyze these transferences they can't do an analysis!

I used to get "good faith" patients who had the balls to work on the cutting edge at the same time I did because they had had combinations of twenty years of two seven year analyses plus several briefer psychotherapies, only to be as crazy as the day they walked in! (- $200,000.00)

As Dr. Donald Rinsley, M.D., fellow-American College of Psychoanalysts wrote about me, my work has both a healing effect and affect. Patients used to pay me six months in advance to hold the time open because I was irreplaceable: I was the only one who could analyze the psychotic core of the personality and I was the only one who could actually do what Dr. Wilfred R. Bion, MRCS (Medical Royal College of Surgeons) wrote about analyzing the psychotic core of the personality.

As I am seventy-six years old, I have written five books that must be read and digested in their entirety. As these books are the thing-in-itself they will transform the reader into the kinds of analyst, patient and psychotherapist who can make a difference in helping people turn the tragic corner in their lives! In other words, these five books are analysis!

These books were written to be around for a few hundred
years and were directly guided by the Almighty!

5 Books Published in 2019 Amazon.com

1. I am Freud! Psychoanalysis is the Only Method of Cure; It's Too Bad No One Knows How To Do One!!!
2. Reverse Analysis, The Existential Shift, Gestalt Family Therapy and The Prevention Of The Next Holocaust

3.   The Art Of Psychotherapy And The Liberation Of The Therapist
4.   The Essence Of Music
5.   ??? The Handbook ???
     ???45 due by 12/01/2019

I Am Freud!

Psychoanalysis Is the Only
Method of Cure:
It's Too Bad No One
Knows How to Do One!!!

Justice is the balancing of Karmic law-natural law-civil law

DR. LEN BERGANTINO, ED.D., PH.D.

"This is a book for all time. As I had extrasensory perception to help me find out things on a primitive level and depth with an ability to pick up split-off, severe pathological projective identifications moment to moment in an era when psychologists were only permitted to be research psychoanalysts by the American Psychoanalytic Association (but tightly controlled where that research was going that in many ways nullified it as true psychoanalytic research), I present to you a book that might at that time have been considered wild psychoanalysis. And I will show you how extrasensory perception can be developed and utilized by the therapeutic use of self within the psychoanalytic frame in ways that can enhance the treatment of borderline, narcissistic, obsessive-compulsive, and schizophrenic disorders and other diagnoses, as well as help pinpoint psychophysiological awareness, which through the repetition compulsion, can prevent disease and will circumvent disease in later life. This kind of psychoanalysis will go a long way in preventing the next holocaust!

Dr. Bergantino and his two children were sent back on a karmic mission to complete the work. Dr. Bergantino is the reincarnated soul of Sigmund Freud and Julius Caesar. Those skill sets were required to complete this project. His children are Wilfred Bion and Milton Erickson. They taught Dr. Bergantino how to use paranormal abilities. We are all off the karmic wheel and WE WILL NOT BE BACK!!! GOODBYE!!!

TO PURCHASE THIS 502 pp. BOOK GO TO www.Xlibris.com and type in either the title of the book or. Dr. Len Bergantino.

I DARED TO DISTURB THE UNIVERSE!!!

Dr. Len Bergantino Ed. D., PhD., releases 'I AM Freud! Psychoanalysis Is the Only Method of Cure: It's Too Bad No One Knows How to Do One!!!"

BEVERLY HILLS, Calif. - Dr. Len Bergantino, Ed.D., Ph.D., is the reincarnated soul of Sigmund Freud and Julius Caesar and his children Lisa Francesca is the reincarnated soul of the great British psychoanalyst Wilfred R. Bion and Cleopatra while his developmentally delayed son Alexander Leonardo is the reincarnated soul of Milton H. Erickson, M.D. (known as the father of Modern Medical Hypnosis and for Uncommon Therapy) and Decimus Brutus. All of those skill sets were necessary in the writing of "I Am Freud! Psychoanalysis is the Only Method of Cure: It's Too Bad No One Knows How to Do One!!!" (published by Xlibris) and the issues it is meant to deal with at both conscious and unconscious levels.

Furthur, Bergatino in 1980, made a direct contact with God to have Bion and Erickson sent back as the reincarnated souls of his children to teach him what to do with the paranormal gifts that were given to him and unleashed by Erickson. Through this development, he, with God's tutelage became the best psychoanalyst that ever lived and began to implement Freud's plan that both psychoanalysis and subsequently developed psychotherapies would create the kind of patients who would and could then go out and create an upward spiraling society.

Wilhelm Reich, M.D. - Freud's most gifted training analyst said "If you can't do politics, you can't do analysis!" The book shows how to develop extrasensory perception so that analysts and therapists have an opportunity to develop the tools necessary to do the jobs at hand if they are so inclined. In this way, people will not pay for a five day a week, seven year analysis and come out as crazy as the day they began with few if any tools to carry on the work. "When I did an analysis with the crème de la crème of society, they customarily tripled their income and the quality of their life! (Don't waste $50,000 per year or $350,000 per analysis)."

The book is not based on anything Bergantino may or may not believe. It is based on his attaining a level of "pure being" that Jean Paul Sartre wrote about as the thing-in-itself. And it is at that level that this book was written as the thing-in-itself to effect change in the reader.

"I Am Freud! Psychoanalysis Is the Only Method of Cure: It's Too Bad No One Knows How to Do One!!!

By Dr. Len Bergatino, Ed.D., Ph.D.
Hardcover | 6 x 9in | 504 pages | ISBN 9781984557308
Softcover | 6 x 9in | 504 pages | ISBN 9781984557292
E-Book | 504 pages | ISBN 9781984557285
Available at www.amazon.com and www.barnesandnoble.com

About the Author

Dr. Len Bergatino, Ed.D., Ph.D. practiced psychoanalysis in Beverly Hills, California from 1979-1991. He saw seven patients five days a week for between five and seven years totaling 49 hours a week and saw an occasional family therapy or clinical hypnosis case totaling 52 hours a week at $125 per hour; $625 per week; $240,000 per year. In addition, he trained psychiatrists and clinical psychologists at the international level delivering on his workshop promise "The Therapheutic Wizardry of Dr. Len Bergantino" at Wentworth Castle in Sheffield, England and training the British at the Royal College of Medicine in London in "Developing the Use of Extrasensory Perception in the Practice of Psychoanalysis, Psychotherapy and Clinical Hypnosis." In Brisbane, Australia, his work was described as "a kind of mental precision" that electrified the Australian Therapeutic Community and had lasting therapeutic impact. Furthermore, he was an affiliate of the Italian American Lawyers Association for seven years. He became an expert witness in both severe parental Alienation Syndrome in criminal cases. He was the only clinician to plea bargain a man for release who was on death row. He was President of the Southern California Society of Clinical Hypnosis when they were composed of exclusively MD's, PHD's and DDS'. The year he was president he turned it into a psychoanalytic institute.

The purpose of this book is to open up the space so that ??? society at large, psychotherapists and patients might ??? LIFE FORCE AND THE THERAPEUTIC USE OF SELF IN CREATING A SOCIETY THAT IS UPWARD SPIRALING INSTEAD OF ONE DOMINATED BY INCURABLE DEATH FORCE! FOR THIS TO HAPPEN. SOCIETY AT LARGE MUST LEARN TO THINK AND PAY ATTENTION TO THE FACTS ON THIS BOOK THAT WILL PERMIT THE CREATION OF NEW THOUGHT TO MEET NEW PROBLEMS; SO THAT WE DO NOT HAVE SITUATIONS LIKE 122 VETERANS A DAY COMMITTING SUICIDE WITHOUT HOPE THAT THERE ARE ANY TREATMENTS FOR THEM NOW OR THAT CAN BE CREATED! IT IS RECOMMENDED THAT THIS BOOK BE READ AS ONE OF A SERIES OF FOUR WRITTEN BY DR. LEN BERGANTINO TO CREATE THIS NEW SOCIETY! WHILE PSYCHOTHERAPY IS THE MEDIUM OF CHOICE IN TH THIS BOOK, THE FOURTH BOOK UTILIZES MUSIC AS THE MEDIUM TO ANSWER SHAKESPEARE'S QUESTIONS TO BE OR NOT TO BE!!!!!!!!!!!!!!!!!!!!!

My Children and I were sent back on a karmic mission to PREVENT THE APOCALYPSE AND WE HAVE DONE OUR PART IN WRITING OUR BOOKS. OW IT IS UP TO YOU TO READ AND UTILIZE THEM. GOD HAS MYSTERIOUSLY MURDERED THREE PERSONS WHO COULD HAVE STOPPED ME FROM FULFILLING THIS MISSION! WE HAVE SUCCEEDED! THE REST IS UP TO YOU OR YOUR ROOMS WILL BE RESERVED IN HELL! Twelve out of 100 million make it into Heaven!

One session existential shift in life long personality characteristic - Both individual and family!

Dr. Len Bergantino, Ed.D., Ph.D., addresses
societal issues in new book

'Reverse Analysis, the Existential Shift, Gestalt Family Therapy and the Prevention of the Next Holocaust' released

LOS ANGELES - Through the Holy Spirit, his direct contact with God and his karmic mission, Dr. Len Bergantino, Ed.D., Ph.D., addresses the problem of the today's downward spiraling society in his latest book "Reverse Analysis, the Existential Shift, Gestalt Family Therapy and the Prevention of the Next Holocaust" (published by Xlibris).

This book creates a subliminal methodology that will help to prevent the next holocaust and perhaps deter the apocalypse and the end of days. As such, the book expands and enriches the community standards of practice of Psychoanalysis, psychiatry, clinical psychology, politics, political intervention and a realliance of religion with the state, as opposed to a separation of church and state that has left its people a soulless and emotionally bankrupt nation with a downward spiraling society. This book throws the United States government and its citizens into an international pot of family therapy as evoked at the unconscious and primitive levels required to effect and affect societal change, to evoke a redirection to an upward spiraling society providing the kind of leadership for Americans to create well-being and prosperity for all.

"[The book] is the common man's best shot to turn the tragic corner in his or her life: make dysfunctional families functional; save one's soul; become thoughtful members of society who do the right thing more often than not," Bergantino says. "This book also trains therapists how to do one session existential shifts thereby creating one to three sessions, ability to function in families and individual, therapies for the common man that are more affordable than a seven year psychoanalysis where the patient is seen five days a week. In other words, it makes the currently impossible possible!"

At its core, the book aims to remind readers to "Open up the space and keep it open so Man will not destroy himself via the illusion of safety and will learn to experientially tolerate the anxiety and chaos of not knowing."

"Reverse Analysis, the Existential Shift, Gestalt Family Therapy and the Prevention of the Next Holocaust"

By Dr. Len Bergantino, Ed.D., Ph.D.
Hardcover | 6 x 9in | 244 pages | ISBN 9781796021189
Softcover | 6 x 9in | 244 pages | ISBN 9781796021172
E-Book | 244 pages | ISBN 9781796021165
Available at Amazon and Barnes & Noble

About the Author

Dr. Len Bergantino, Ed.D., Ph.D., has written THE HOLY BIBLE OF Psychoanalysis, psychotherapy, political psychology and music-books, I-IV!!! The books are the thing-in-itself and all four books must be read to make the necessary personal and societal impact!!! He was trained by Milton Erickson, M.D., Carl Whitaker, M.D., Wilfred Bion, M.R.C.S., Walter Kempler, M.D., George Bach, Ph.D., Bruno Bettelheim, Ph.D., Jim Simkin, Ph.D., and Erv Polsters, Ph.D., they had the most lasting impact along with the Holy Spirit. Bergantino is the author of "The Essence of Music," "The Art of Psychotherapy and the Liberation of the Therapist," "I Am Freud! Psychoanalysis Is the Only Method of Cure: It's Too Bad No One Knows How to Do One!!!," "Reverse Analysis, the Existential Shift, Gestalt Family Therapy and the Prevention of the Next Holocaust," "Psychotherapy, Insight, and Style: The Existential Moment", and "Making an Impact in Therapy: How Master Clinicians Intervene."

The Art *of*
Psychotherapy
And the **Liberation**
of the **Therapist**

*Much has been written about the Science of Psychotherapy, but
it has remained for Dr. Bergantino to write about the Art of
Psychotherapy with such elegant impact.*

Dr. Len Bergantino, Ed.D., Ph.D.

This is a book for professional psychotherapists, psychoanalysts, and counselors; students in those areas of specialty; and lay persons who are interested in the essence of effective therapy and how some of the people who do it best practice their art. For professionals, the book presents a personal way of viewing therapy that can add pleasurable options. Each of the therapists with whom I worked, and myself, all had a feeling of enjoyment that we hope will carry over to the office and practices of the readers. For students of therapy, the book offers a search for a professional stature and working posture that may be of value in the development of each student's unique personal style. For lay persons, the book speaks of therapy that can make an impact and speaks of how some of the most potent therapists practice. For Psychoanalysts interested in the work of the Great British Psychoanalyst, Dr. Wilfred R. Bion MRCS (Medical Royal College of Surgeons), This is the only book that demonstrates exactly what he did.

I wrote the book with the intention of having it be both an experience and an explanation. I have presented it according to my developmental needs while maturing personally and professionally. This was done so the book might be informative at the conscious level, entertaining at the child level, and persuasive at the unconscious level.

The existential moment is the thread that ties the book together; it is a moment of therapeutic potency. While all moments are existential by definition, there are certain moments that are more powerful in helping patients live happier and healthier lives. Positive results, whether they be from one session or over the long haul, are partially, if not fully, a result of existential moments.

Book shares the art of effective therapy and the political conditions required for patients and therapist to make its practice safe for both

Dr. Len Bergantino, Ed.D., Ph.D. releases "The Art of Psychotherapy and the Liberation of the Therapist'

LOS ANGELES - Dr. Len Bergantino, Ed.D., Ph.D., stated today, there are careful psychotherapists who do not have the courage to take risks to develop the therapeutic use of self to the degree that they can break new ground. For him, these things keep the field of psychothcrapy from advancing to the point where it can meet most of the new challenges of the times. Thus, Bergantino writes "The Art of Psychotherapy and the Liberation of the "Therapist" (published by Xlibris).

This is a book for professional psychotherapists, psychoanalysts and counselors, students in those areas of specialty and laypersons who are interested in the essence of effective therapy and how some of the people who do it best practice their art. For professionals, the book presents a personal way of viewing therapy that can add pleasurable options. Each of the therapists with whom Bergantino worked, and himself, all had a feeling of enjoyment that they hope will carry over to the office and practices of the readers. For students of therapy, the book offers a search for a professional stature and working posture that may be of value in the development of each student's unique personal style. For laypersons, the book speaks of therapy that can make an impact and speaks of how some of the most potent therapists practice.

The chapter and the work of Dr. Wilfred R. Bion, the Great British Psychoanalyst, is the only place ever written where you can actually read Bion doing 12 hours of audio tape supervisions with the young M.D. in analytic training plus the work of some of Bion's best Analysands and M.D. Training and Supervisor Analyst.

"I wrote the book with the intention of having it be both an experience and an explanation. I have presented it according to my developmental needs while maturing personally and professionally. This was done so the book might be informative at the conscious level, entertaining at the child level and persuasive at the unconscious level," Bergantino says.

Bergantino adds, "The existential moment is the thread that ties the book together; it is a moment of therapeutic potency. While all moments are existential by definition, there are certain moments that are more powerful in helping patients live happier and healthier lives. Positive results, whether they be from one session or over the long haul, are partially, if not fully, a result of existential moments."

"The Art of Psychotherapy and the Liberation of the Therapist"
By Dr. Len Bergantino, Ed.D., Ph.D.
Hardcover | 6 x 9in | 596 pages | ISBN 9781796024234
Softcover | 6 x 9in | 596 pages | ISBN 9781796024227
E-Book | 596 pages | ISBN 9781796024210
Available at Amazon and Barnes & Noble

About the Author

Dr. Len Bergantino, Ed.D., Ph.D. practiced psychoanalysis in Beverly Hills, California from 1979-1991. He saw seven patients five days a week for between five and seven years totaling 49 hours a week and saw an occasional family therapy or clinical hypnosis case totaling 52 hours a week at $125 per hour; $625 per week; $240,000 per year. In addition, he trained psychiatrists and clinical psychologists at the international level delivering on his workshop promise "The Therapeutic Wizardry of Dr. Len Bergantino" at Wentworth Castle in Sheffield, England and training the British at the Royal College of Medicine in London in "Developing the Use of Extrasensory Perception in the Practice of Psychoanalysis, Psychotherapy and Clinical Hypnosis." In Brisbane, Australia, his work was described as "a kind of mental precision" that electrified the Australian Therapeutic Community and had lasting therapeutic impact". Furthermore, he was an affiliate of the Italian American Lawyers Association for seven years. He became an expert witness in both Severe Parental Alienation Syndrome in criminal cases. He was the only clinical psychologist in the history of the State of California to plea bargain a man for release who was on death row. He was President of the Southern California Society of Clinical Hypnosis when they were composed of exclusively MD's, PHD's and DDS'. The year he was president he turned it into a psychoanalytic institute.

Music is the international language, but what is music!?!!?

For The Bergantino Bredice Family Music was the FAMILY BUSINESS!

My father, Dan Bergantino, always told me, (in terms of what kind of music you listen to) "IF YOU PUT SHIT IN, SHIT WILL COME OUT! (WHEN YOU PLAY MUSIC)

My cousin Louis Bredice told me, "When I first started playing Jazz, I played a lot of notes! Then I realized, all I needed were the right ones!"

My cousin Freddie Bredice had the faster technique on guitar I had ever seen! The first time I met him was on a gig in 1967. His speed was blinding, faster than a speeding bullet! I was leaning against a wooden beam next to him and when he finished I said, "You must be cousin Fred!" He said, "Yeah, I don't play chords! It fucks up your hands! "Freddie was one of Joe Diori's guitar teachers and Joe said he still has nightmares about Freddie's speed! Joe was known as the best jazz guitar player in the world among guitar players. I got him to play songs again in a cd entitled "FALLING IN LOVE" where I am playing mandolin and Joe is accompanying me on guitar. This cd can be purchased from orchard records.com and amazon.com. On the top picture: USA BERGANTINO (left), DR. LEN BERGANTINO (middle), and ALEX BERGANTINO (right).

This is a multi-purpose book in that much as a previously published book entitled "ZEN AND THE ART OF MOTORCYCLE MAINTENANCE" had more to do with human growth than motorcycle maintenance; this book is a natural model of how musicians as human beings deal with each other thereby providing a baseline for humans in answering Shakespeare's question, "TO BE OR NOT TO BE!" FURTHER, THIS BOOK IS SUBSTANTIVE AND DEPTHFUL ENOUGH TO BE USED IN MUSIC SCHOOLS, NO MATTER WHAT MUSIC GENRE, IN THAT IT FOCUSES ON MUSICALITY, PURE SOUND, THE ART OF MELODY AND PEACE' AND IT CAN BE UTILIZED IN THE PSYCHOTHERAPEUTIC ARTS AND ITS CONTENTS ARE HEALING IN NATURE!

THE REVEREND DR. LEN BERGANTINO
PROFESSIONAL MUSICIAN FROM 1996-2012
(AGE 56-70) MUSICIAN'S LOCAL, 47
AMERICAN FEDERATION OF MUSICIAN'S

Dr. Len Bergantino, Ed.D., Ph.D., reveals 'The Essence of Music' in his latest book

*New book focuses on musicality, pure sound, the art of melody
and inner peace to bring out the best in musicians*

LOS ANGELES - People say that music is the international language, but what is music? For Dr. Len Bergantino, Ed.D., Ph.D., music is a family business. However, as a professional psychoanalyst and a professional musician, he sees that the essence of music has become long forgotten by most musicians who now make "noise" and call it "music." Hence, in latest publication titled "The Essence of Music" (published by Xlibris), the author intends to reverse this process.

Coming from a family of musicians, it is not a surprise that Bergantino was introduced to the world of music at a young age. In an entertaining and evocative style, he offers readers the depths and substance of what he learned from some of the best musicians in the world, as well as psychoanalysis and in direct contact with the Holy Spirit, which found a way to have musicians play music from the inside out so they are not merely playing technical notes.

"The Essence of Music" is a multi-purpose book that serves as a natural model for how musicians, as human beings, deal with each other, thereby providing a baseline for humans in answering Shakespeare's question, "To be or not to be." Furthermore, the book is substantive and full of depth, enough to be used in music schools no matter what musical genre since it focuses on musicality, pure sound, the art of melody and inner peace. It can be utilized in the psychotherapeutic arts, and its content is healing in nature.

Bergantino adds that at its core, the publication of "The Essence of Music" intends to invade the unconscious minds of people and musicians in bettering themselves. "I want readers to not only play and appreciate music from the source of his or her inner being but to transmit that source to the way he or she lives life in creating an upward spiraling society," Bergantino adds.

"The Essence of Music: Musicality, Pure Sound, the Art of Melody and Inner Peace"
By Dr. Len Bergantino, Ed.D., Ph.D.

Hardcover | 6 x 9in | 284 pages | ISBN 9781796029178
Softcover | 6 x 9in | 284 pages | ISBN 9781796029161
E-Book | 284 pages | ISBN 9781796029154
Available at Amazon and Barnes & Noble

MY FIFTH BOOK PUBLISHED BETWEEN NOVEMBER, 2018 AND NOVEMBER 2019 IS ENTITLED <u>SANCTIMONIOUS PSYCHOPROCTOLOGICAL INVASIONS: THE HANDBOOK FOR POLITICAL ANALYSIS</u>

Publisher Rose Dog Books ISBN # 978-1-6461-0238-9

While 5 of my 6 published books from 2019 to 2020 are published by Xlibris Publishing Company uner website name of Dr. Len Bergantino. com <u>SANCTIMONIOUS PSYCHOPROCTOLOGICAL INVASIONS: THE HANDBOOK FOR POLITICAL ANALYSIS</u> WAS PUBLISHED BY ROSE DOG BOOKS, A PART OF DORRANCE PUBLISHING COMPANY UNDER THE NAME "<u>THE REVEREND DR.</u> LEN BERGANTINO, ED.D., (USC); Ph.D., D.Div., <u>POLITICAL ANALYST</u>

***This book was written for THE UNDESERVING POOR as well as professions who need to make a professional impact to effectively serve the public while my particular areas of expertise are psychoanalysis, the art and CLINICAL WISDOM of Psychotherapy, Music, Education and Religion, this book transcends those areas of expertise in showing the public WHAT WAS DONE AND WHAT IS REQUIRED TO MAKE AN IMPACT UPON THE SYSTEM AS A WHOLE IN STATE AND LOCAL AS WELL AS INTERNATIONAL POLITICAL CULTURES!

<u>TO BUY THIS BOOK</u> (1) Email bookorders @ rosedogbooks.com or (2) call 1-800-788-7654 between 8 am and 5 pm Eastern Standard Time.

ABOUT THE AUTHOR: This book is a political statement of my own in it's entirety. It demonstrates how the NATURAL ORDER OF PERSONAL DEVELOPMENT HAS CHANNELED ALL OF MY SKILLS PREVIOUSLY UTILIZED IN PSYCHOANALYSIS, CLINICAL PSYCHOLOGY, PSYCHOTHERAPY, MUSIC, EDUCATION AND RELIGION. THIS IS A BOOK ABOUT HOW TO DO THE RIGHT THING AND GET AWAY WITH IT!

The Reverend Dr. Len Bergantino
Political Analyst

About the Author

D r. Len Bergantino, Ed.D., Ph.D., went from being a professional psychoanalyst to a professional musician at the age of 56. He has developed an international reputation in both areas through his four books which are divinely inspired by the Holy Spirit to at the very least give men and women an opportunity to be more fully themselves and more in touch with their own nature. His collection includes "I AM FREUD! Psychoanalysis Is the Only Method of Cure: It's Too Bad No One Knows How to Do One!!!," "Reverse Analysis, the Existential Shift, Gestalt Family Therapy and the Prevention of the Next Holocaust," "The Art of Psychotherapy and the Liberation of the Therapist" and "The Essence of Music." To know more details about the author and his works, visit www.drlenbergantino.com.

The Reverend Dr. Len Bergantino, Ed.D., Ph.D.

From 2012 through 2018, Len Bergantino began each day with pro bono writings and invasive interventions that insist and expand upon the first amendment rights of United States citizens. In all areas, he is both knowledgeable and feels national, state, and local governments are stuck in socially immobile positions. He created ways to invade entire cultures and governments to move those stuck in quicksand off the dime and into a society that spirals upward. He refers to the creation of these methods as sanctimonious psychoproctological invasions in the creation of a political psychology that should be studies by all human beings who want to make a difference and give meaning to their lives.

Sanctimonious Psychoproctological Invasions: The Handbook for Political Analysis

Len Bergantino is a multi-faceted individual who achieved international prominence in the areas of psychoanalysis, psychotherapy, clinical psychology, and music. His other fields include education and religion, with a precursory knowledge of medicine and law. He is a weathervane in terms of knowing the right thing to do and has the temperament of Che Guevarra in getting it done!

The Reverend Dr. Len Bergantino, Ed.D. (USC), Ph.D., D. Div. Political Analyst

To order a copy of ***Sanctimonious Psychoproctological Invasions*** Email **bookorders@rosedogbooks.com** or call **1-800-788-7654**

DR. LEN BERGANTINO - EDUCATIONAL CONSULTANT
Educational Storytelling - *The Best Since Mark Twain and Will Rogers*
(310) 207-9397

PRESS RELEASE   "WHEN BASEBALL WAS KING

THE NEW YORK YANKEES WERE KING OF BASEBALL"

Perhaps Allie Reynolds best summed it up when the New York
Yankees bought him from the Cleveland Indians and he was asked
"What is the difference pitching for cleveland as opposed to
The New York Yankees?" He said, "I am a Cherokee Indian from
Oklahoma. In Cleveland they call me copperhead and old
blanket ass! In New York they call me The Super Chief!
That's the difference!" The New York Yankees won five
world series in a row! (1949-1953)

This book contains the folklore of baseball in an era that not
only achieved EXCELLENCE but produced a quality of athlete
that became party of your family at the dinner table!

It is an era the spirit of place of which should be remembered;
even those who played against the Yankees and provided a good
deal of torture to Yankee fans! For example, one of the
highlights for me in writing this book was in getting to
know and talk with Carl Erskine, the Brooklyn Dodger who in
the third game of the 1953 world series pitched the most
dominant game I ever saw pitched against what many consider to
be the best baseball team in the history of baseball. He
struck out 14 Yankees, and Mickey Mantle four times on that
day!

Doctor of Education - University of Southern California
1215 Brockton Avenue, Suite 104, Los Angeles, California 90025

I, CARL ERSKINE HEREBY GRANT DR. LEN BERGANTINO AND

X1IBRIS PUBLISHING COMPANY THE RIGHT TO USE A PICTURE

OF MICKEY MANTLE PERSONALLY SIGNED TO ME FOR USE IN HIS

UPCOMING BOOK.   THIS PHOTO IS IN MY BOOK, "TALES FROM

THE DODGER DUGOUT", PAGE 148 (from my personal

collection).

THIS AUTHORIZATION IS GRANTED ON FEBRUARY 7, 2020.

CARL ERSKINE

BROOKLYN, LOS ANGELES DODGERS

This photo was given to me by the Mick himself. *(Courtesy of Mickey Mantle)*

DR. LEN BERGANTINO - CLINICAL PSYCHOLOGY
Diplomate in Family Psychology
American Board of Professional Psychology
Trained by Carl Whitaker, M.D. in Telephonic Family Therapy

TO HIRE ME AS A CONSULTANT
CALL (424) 293-9511
(7 RINGS)

In March, 2020, Carl Erskine who played for the Brooklyn Dodgers said he met and played against Jimmy Piersall and the Boston Red Sox once in Spring Training. Erskine said Piersall got a double, then called time out, and walked to the mound asking Erskine if he wanted "his autograph". Piersall was the most colorful baseball player I saw during my era.

REV. DR. LEN BERGANTINO
PRIME MINISTER - UNIV. LIFE CHURCH - WLA
ED.D. (USC - 1971) DOCTOR OF EDUCATION
Ph.D. (INT'L. COLLEGE - 1977) CLINICAL PSYCH.

All Long Distance calls for Family Therapy from Hawaii
paid for by Dr. Bergantino.
1215 Brockton Avenue, Suite 104, Los Angeles, California 90025

To Lew
Dr. Lew
17
Carl Erskine
1948-1957
Dodgers

A message from:

Carl Erskine   Nov 2, '20

HELLO DR. LEN,

YOU HAVE SENT ME MANY CORSPONDENCES AND I THANK YOU. BETTY AND I HAVE ENJOYED THE FRUIT BASKET — AND IT'S LASTED OVER TIME. —

WE ARE DOING WELL IN OUR VILLA — BOTH RESONABLY HEALTHY FOR 90 PLUS. —

WE CHEERED HARD FOR THE DODGERS. —

WE SEND OUR BEST

Betty & Carl Erskine

No Hit Cubs   **No Hit N.Y. Giants**   **World Series**
"K" Record 14 vs N.Y. Yankees

Last out baseballs from each game, courtesy of Hall of Fame, Museum
Carl Erskine, Brooklyn, L.A. Dodgers 1948 - 1959

A message from:
Carl Erskine   Mar 17, 2020

Dr. Len, —

          Since you attended
Ebbets Field Oct. 2, 1953
and have written in
such elegant ways
about that record game,
I'm sending you a
picture I've only shared
with my family.
                    Regards,
                    Carl Erskine

This photo was given to me by the Mick himself. (Courtesy of
Mickey Mantle)

The Reverend Dr. Len Bergantino is a multi-faceted individual who achieved international prominence in the areas of psychoanalysis, psychotherapy, clinical psychology, and music. His other fields include education and religion, with a precursory knowledge of medicine and law. He is a weathervane in terms of knowing the right thing to do and has the temperament of Che Guevarra in getting it done!

When the Reverend Dr. Len Bergantino grew up, the first thing he had in mind was to wear number 22 and take over for Allie Reynolds, the Super Chief, as the Mainstay of the Mound Staff of the NEW YORK YANKEES!!! The New York Yankees won 5-world series in a row. (1949-1953) !!!

No Hit Cubs   No Hit N.Y. Giants   World Series
                                                 "K" Record 14 vs N.Y. Yankees

Last out baseballs from each game, courtesy of Hall of Fame, Museum
Carl Erskine, Brooklyn, L.A. Dodgers 1948 - 1959

To Gene
Dr. Gene
17
Carl Erskine
1948 - 1957
Dodgers

When Baseball was King the New York Yankees were King of Baseball

The Reverend Dr. Len Bergantino is a multi-faceted individual who achieved international prominence in the areas of psychoanalysis, psychotherapy, clinical psychology, and music. His other fields include education and religion, with a precursory knowledge of medicine and law. He is a weathervane in terms of knowing the right thing to do and has the temperament of Che Guevarra in getting it done!

When the Reverend Dr. Len Bergantino grew up, the first thing he has in mind Was to wear number 22 and take over for Allie Reynolds, the Super Chief, as the Mainstay of the Mound Staff of the NEW YORK YANKEES!!! The New York Yankees won 5-world series in a row. (1949 - 1953)!!!